THE STARS MY BLANKET

Beryl Boxer Smeeton in Kochi dress, Powindah, northern India.

THE STARS MY BLANKET

Beryl Smeeton

Horsdal & Schubart

Horsdal & Schubart Publishers Ltd.
Victoria, B.C., Canada

Cover photograph by Carole Sabiston, Victoria, B.C.

Photographs in the text are from the collection of Clio Smeeton, Cochrane, Alberta.

Maps from *High Endeavours* by Miles Clark, © 1991, published by Douglas & McIntyre. Reprinted by permission.

This book is set in New Baskerville Book Text.

Printed and bound in Canada by Hignell Printing Limited, Winnipeg.

Canadian Cataloguing in Publication Data

Smeeton, Beryl 1905-1979
Winter shoes in springtime

ISBN 0-920663-38-9

1. Smeeton, Beryl 1905-1979. 2. Travelers—Biography. I. Title.
G490.S63 1995   910'.92   C95-910277-9

FOREWORD

B ERYL Smeeton's approach to life had no room for restrictions; instead, she lived by a mixture of cautious pragmatism and unbridled enthusiasm. She was a woman of many contradictions, who nonetheless stood by principles as firmly grounded as the Rocky Mountains which overlook the house she and Miles built in the wild, rolling foothills of Alberta, where they are both buried.

Beryl was born on September 21, 1905, at Tolpuddle, Dorset, into a grand Edwardian world which still reflected the golden tranquillity, stability and power that was the British Empire. Hers was the classic childhood of that period and class, of stately homes, of nannies, of listening to her mother "do her bit for the troops" by warbling "My Little Grey Home in the West". Beryl loved her Nanny more dearly than her elegant, seldom-seen, Australian mother.

Governed by the myriad rules of this girlhood, she yearned to escape. She obeyed the dictates of her class, if not her heart, by marrying as was expected of her, into the military hierarchy which was her parents' *mileu*. That marriage was the last nod she gave to convention. It did not provide the independence she craved but turned out to be an unworkable predicament which, finally, she left.

Once gone, she rarely looked back. She plunged joyfully into every adventure that offered, and by the time she was in her late 20s she had trekked alone across four continents, something which, at that time, very few men, let alone single women, were attempting. Until the mid-1960s Beryl held the world's height record for women for mountain climbing without oxygen.

Yet, much as she wanted to escape her aristocratic upbringing, it had marked her, not only in her stoic grace and courage under

trying circumstances, but also in the gaiety, elegance and efferves-
cent wit illustrated by the clothes she wore — silk shirts, scarves
and pearls beneath worn demin coveralls and a rawhide waistcoat
with elkhorn buttons.

In the 1930s she found a soulmate in Miles Smeeton, and
together they climbed, sailed and adventured until her death in
1979. Though Miles has written about their sometimes hair-
raising exploits in his own many books, *Winter Shoes in Springtime*
and *The Stars My Blanket* are Beryl's story, without Miles. They
echo with happiness and with the excitement of vividly experi-
enced freedom.

Sprague Theobald
Yacht *Gryphon*
Offshore Los Angeles

CONTENTS

Map from HIGH ENDEAVOURS by Miles Clark.

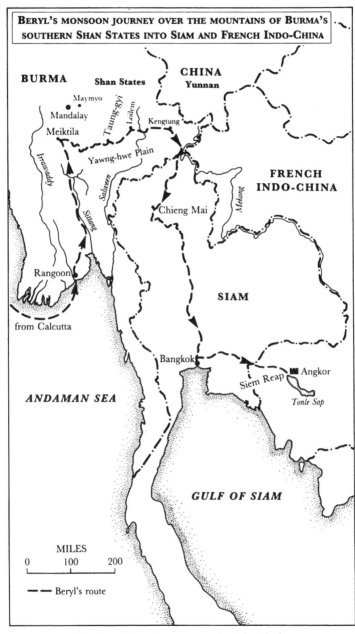

Map from High Endeavours by Miles Clark.

To Miles, who bought me the typewriter

INTRODUCTION

I FIRST met Beryl in India, when she came to Poona. Her husband, who was 14 years older than she was, had been posted as Second-in-Command to my regiment. She was a vibrant, enthusiastic young woman, bringing light and laughter wherever she went. Her golden hair was tightly coiled over her ears, her figure slim and firm. She glowed with health and energy, ready for any adventure that offered excitement and an outpouring of physical effort.

With horses always to be exercised, I took her riding, at which she was virtually a beginner, and when she started hunting with the Poona and Kirkee hounds, she claimed that she was the only woman who ever wore out her riding boots in pursuit of her horse.

Our first climb together was to the top of one of the tall radio masts at Kirkee, where we took a picnic supper to the platform which crowned it and surveyed the world below as from a balloon. She soon became an enthusiastic companion in climbs up the Ghats, the jungle-clad mountains on the west side of the Deccan. She loved to scramble, hatless, up to the old Maharatta forts that topped them, the more direct the route the better. When she arrived, scratched and breathless, with clothing torn, she used to cool off by plunging in her clothes into the old reservoirs that once supplied the forts and which were now filled with stinking water and green weed.

Most of all, Beryl loved to swim across any lake or river that she might discover. She swam like a fish, having learned to swim as a child from many sunlit beaches in Bermuda, where her father, a soldier, had been stationed. Although I was faster than she on the hill, I was by far her inferior in the water and often found myself ploughing across a lake, half a mile behind her, and in considerable doubt as to whether I would make it to the other side.

One day, shortly before I was due to return to England, at the end of my foreign tour, we were riding together, when she asked me how I was going home.

"Oh, I don't know. Second class P. and O., I suppose," I replied. "I can't afford anything else."

"How perfectly awful," she said. "Why don't you go overland? I should love to go overland. You could do it just as cheaply."

In those days, the overland route to India was in no way the hackneyed route that it is today. When we got back from our ride, I went to her house to look at an atlas, and we planned the way that I might go. It was impossible to resist her enthusiasm. A week later, when we were riding again, she pulled up her horse and said to me: "I want to ask you a very serious question."

I could not imagine what might seem serious to her, and I had absolutely no idea that the whole course of my life might hang on my reply. I asked her what it was.

"Beryl loved to swim": an early photograph of Beryl, which Clio Smeeton says her father carried in his wallet all his life.

"Would you mind very much," she asked, "if I came home with you overland? We are going home anyway and Tom says that I may travel with you overland, because he knows that I can't bear to think of you going overland while I go on the ship."

She was the best of companions, in fact the best companion that I had ever had. "Of course," I said, "I would love you to come with me." There was no idea in her mind that such a journey would lead to anything other than the companionship that we had enjoyed. I had been brought up to conform to a certain code, but if I had any doubts about my own ability to keep to it, I had no doubt about hers. There was such trust and confidence, an untouchable innocence in those steady, widely spaced eyes.

We went overland from Basra, travelling third class to Baghdad and then by a lorry, loaded with dried fish and a few Arabs, across the desert to Jerusalem. Then on foot and by local bus through Palestine, Syria and Turkey. We climbed Mount Herman in Syria and Mount Erjias in Turkey, then took deck passage through the Bosphorus to Varna. We walked through the Balkans, then travelled through Romania, Hungary and Czechoslovakia to Germany, where we walked through the Black Forest, travelling always as cheaply as possible and meeting with many people and much kindness.

I cannot say that I, a more or less orthodox army officer, always enjoyed this cheap form of travel, although I loved travelling with someone as exciting as Beryl. She, however, liked to share buses and caravanserai with the common man, no matter how common he was. She thought nothing of bedbugs and fleas, or even lice, which last we were spared. She relished the whole idea of cheap travel. Every day brought a challenge, every penny saved a minor victory. To buy some fly-ridden mutton chop in a local bazaar, to wrap beans in a flabby pancake-like bread, to eat this strange meal and to sleep in the open, to see new countries and to meet and to talk with the local people, this was for her the very essence of life.

Halfway through the journey, we were deeply in love. In love? In Paradise, I thought, walking with a golden girl through the mountains and amongst the flowers, with rucksacks, in which we carried all our needs, on our backs. No past, no future, but only the joy of the day. It had to end and one day we came face to face with the fact that I was a soldier and that she was married to a brother officer. We decided not to meet or to write to each other

xiii

for a year, a compact faithfully kept. Beryl went back to India with her husband, and I, after many restless nights thinking about emigration to Australia, the Foreign Legion, and a job as an airline pilot, went back to soldiering in England. I knew that I would have to leave the regiment and fortunately the opportunity was not far away.

Beryl's next major journey was made after that year was over, an unhappy year for both of us. She left India from Meerut, travelling overland through Persia and Russia, the only person who knew that her marriage was ended. In those days, there was very little travel overland through Persia from India, and none by young women on their own. She narrowly missed the great Quetta earthquake, which occurred just before her arrival there, but she had a knack for getting into exciting things, arriving once in Lisbon to the shot and shell of a revolution, which she thought was some holiday celebration, and in Shanghai as the Japanese fought their way into Chapei, a part of the city. She anticipated no insult, trouble or danger in her travels, and because of this fearlessness and trust, avoided the pitfalls that a more timid woman might have fallen into. Rather, because of her radiance and vitality, she tended to meet interesting and intelligent people, who looked after her and helped her on her way.

During the year that she was in India, I had taken up mountain climbing. Now she joined me in Austria, where we had a climbing holiday, and a very lucky escape, when we had a fall on the Drei Herren Spitze, where some wind-packed snow broke away on a very steep shoulder. This decided Beryl to do some more climbing, so she spent some months in Austria, never at a loss for climbing companions, and at the same time learning to speak German. During one of these climbs, on the Fünf Finger Spitze, in the Dolomites, her companion fell on a difficult pitch and broke his leg. Beryl managed to hold him and luckily they were seen from below by four Germans, who were practising for the North Face of the Eiger. They could not have been discovered by better climbers, who soon came up and brought the injured man down.

Two years after our climbing adventure Beryl decided to cross Russia on the Trans-Siberian railway, travelling with her brother Charles, a soldier, who was on his way to take up an appointment in Hong Kong. He was going to spend Christmas with the Dutch

Ambassador in Tokyo and Beryl was asked too. She returned to Austria for some more climbing and then travelled third class to meet Charles in Moscow, stopping over on the way in Leningrad. From Moscow on to Tokyo, and Christmas with the Ambassador, she travelled first class. She was always able to switch with ease through all levels of society.

On this trip, she undertook a small smuggling job for a Russian *emigré*, taking a book that he had written about the horrors of the revolution and his escape from Russia to his parents, who were unable to leave Harbin. Beryl, indignant that such restrictions should keep a family separate, undertook to take the book to them, but she could have been in serious trouble if she had been caught with it.

After spending some time in Japan, she took ship to Hong Kong and from there did a really remarkable journey, travelling third class like any Chinese peasant. She went by bus to Chengtu and Mount Omei, which she climbed. Then back by boat down the Min River to Chungking. The country was just recovering from the rule of the warlords, who had only recently been subdued by Chiang Kai Shek.

The next part of her journey was again by country bus to Kunming, along a newly constructed road, as Chiang was already securing his communications with Burma in case the Japanese should cut off his communications with the sea. From the roadhead, she then took the old tribute trail on foot to Tali and Tengyueh, and so into Burma to Myitkynar. This was the most hazardous part of the journey, as the country was far from settled and she was warned against kidnappers. Warnings always served as a spur to her intent. Beryl wrote about this journey, and about her travels through Persia and Russia, in a delightful book called *Winter Shoes in Springtime*.

When Beryl reached Myitkynar, the time for my annual two months leave, which was considered necessary for those who had endured the heat of the summer in the Indian Plains, was approaching. She joined me and we walked into Chamba, a small hill state, and explored a high pass over the main Himalayan range into Zaskar, which had not been used for years, nor was it properly surveyed. From Padam, we went south into Lahoul to Kyelang, and then discovered another high and unused pass into Kulu. From Manali, we attempted to take my faltboot down the swift-running Beas River and lost the canoe and almost ourselves when we tried involuntarily to negotiate a waterfall.

Beryl, who had by now obtained a divorce, was unwilling to commit herself to marriage after her first unsuccessful experience. She was enjoying her freedom and I had to content myself with the hope of seeing her from time to time. Her next great journey was undertaken at the instigation of Peter Fleming, and this and one other remarkable solo journey, that she carried out after she had married me, are the subjects of this book. These are accounts of journeys made many years ago, but perhaps not much has changed in some of those areas in all this time. Yet the value of the accounts is not so much in the description of the countries through which she passed and of the people that she met, as in the courage and the zest for life which shine through her writing, which never left her, and for which everyone who ever met her remembers her.

When she married me, it was a tremendous concession on her part, because she was giving up much of the freedom that she had won so painfully. As far as I could, I tried always to preserve it for her, because for no one could these lines be more apt:

> I cannot rest from travel: I will drink
> Life to the lees: All times I have enjoyed
> Greatly, have suffered greatly, both with those
> That loved me and alone; on shore, and when
> Through scudding drifts the rainy Hyades
> Vexed the dim sea.

Miles Smeeton

CHAPTER ONE
BETWEEN THE MAIZE AND THE IMMENSITY

THE letter was headed "The Times. Printing House Square. London." It began: "Dear Madam, we have heard with interest of your journey through China and if you are not averse to publication...."

This, I thought, was my "Open Sesame," particularly the phrase "not averse to publication." In no time my imagination had installed me as a Special Foreign Correspondent to *The Times*. When I presented my handwritten manuscript, I was received by Peter Fleming, who had crossed the Gobi Desert with Ella Maillart and who was the best-mannered man I had ever met. Both of them had written books that were to influence me in my wish to travel to out-of-the-way places.

"Unfortunately, since you terminated your very interesting journey," he told me, "the Chinese and the Japanese have officially declared war on each other and we feel that we cannot publish a lighthearted travelogue about a country while it is at war."

Striving to recover something from the wreck of my hopes, I then asked if travel in any other part of the world would interest *The Times'* readers. Peter Fleming was not prepared to commit himself and asked where I was thinking of going.

"To South America," I replied, having just finished reading *The Conquest of Peru* by Prescott, but I said it almost without thinking.

"Well, we might be interested in the rumour of a lost city at the bottom of the Andes, and anything new you might find out about the mylodon."

Prescott had not mentioned the mylodon, but I had heard about the lost city, last hiding-place of the Incas. The mylodon was a kind of prehistoric cow that had been found by some gauchos in a cave in Patagonia, and now he told me that there had been rumours of an unknown tribe, not too far away, in the southern Cordillera.

I left the office with nothing more than an attractive-looking document stating that *The Times* had asked me to find out more about rumours of a lost tribe in the Cordillera. But there was no mention of money, nor even any promise to accept any article I might write. But still, it looked very impressive to me, and, in due course, had a galvanic effect on some of the lesser-educated South Americans.

I went down to Dorset, where my brother Charles was living, my head full of images of tropical jungles, and began to assemble my clothes for the journey. Charles asked me what I was doing, and when I showed him *The Times* letter, merely observed that he did not think I should need any summer clothes in Patagonia.

"If you don't believe me, look it up in the *Encyclopaedia Britannica*," he said, and I hurried down to the library to look it up in the old edition that had belonged to my Grandmother. "Patagonia is a pebbly desert, interspersed with lakes of Epsom salts" was what I learned. At least that would save me taking my Fructines Vichy, I thought to myself. Back in London, I decided that my best route would be to fly as far as I could. It was already the end of October, and, if I wanted to reach the Straits of Magellan in time for the short Patagonian summer, I should certainly have to be there by the end of December at the latest.

Booking a seat on a French plane flying to Dakar in French Equatorial Africa was fairly easy, and from there, I secured a steerage passage on an Italian liner going to Rio and Buenos Aires. Getting the necessary visas for Brazil, Argentina and Chile, however, was less simple and new to me. It involved endless written questionnaires (some of a particularly rude personal nature), fingerprints and medical certificates, not to mention quite large sums of money.

Since obtaining a divorce, I had reverted to my maiden name, and even a very limited acquaintance with South American men in St. Jean de Luz would have prompted me to travel in their countries as an English miss, rather than as a divorcee, but I had some trouble with the authorities when I went to get my new passport in my old name. I was summoned to the room of a very serious official, who courteously explained, "It is impossible to become a spinster again after you have been married." However, as a great concession, he finally agreed to leave out the Mrs. and to issue it with no prefix, simply under Beryl Boxer.

It was piercingly cold when I left London a couple of weeks later. I was warmly dressed and carried introductions to a big firm of frozen meat exporters. When we touched down briefly in Government Spain, then well into their second year of Civil War, I was already beginning to feel the heat. It was a tiny airport, with nothing but a few petrol drums and a patched tent, where they offered us a brew which they called coffee. The officials were in rags, and hunger was stamped on their faces, but they behaved with such unconscious dignity that I, too hot and too well-fed, felt quite abashed in their presence.

By the time we got to Casablanca, I was starving. In 1937, air services outside Europe tended to be makeshift, and there was neither hostess nor any form of refreshment on board. The other passengers, all Frenchmen, were as famished as I. For an unknown reason, we were not allowed through a barrier to a cafe where some of the Casablancans were sitting in the twilight, enjoying satisfying snacks. In the end, another desperate passenger and I climbed a fence and rushed over to the cafe, but we only managed to get some bread and a couple of eggs, and were half-way through them when an irate official arrived to escort us back to the plane. The other passengers, already seated, gazed enviously at the rolls clutched in our hands.

As we flew towards the equator, the heat began to seep in despite the altitude, and by the time the plane touched down at Dakar aerodrome, I was sweating freely.

The heat was suffocating. As we stepped out of the plane, it was as though an oven door had been opened. Various officials and Customs men were standing about in the moonlight, and despite the temperature and the lateness of the hour, my appearance — the only woman on the plane — caused general consternation. An official advanced upon me to enquire, anxiously, whether I was travelling alone. When I said "Yes" his concern and embarrassment grew, while he studied a pink form that he held.

"There is an epidemic in the Interior," he explained, "and all the hotels are full. Of course, I was notified of the number of air passengers, but not of their sex, and I have only just managed to get enough beds by putting three or four in a room." By this time, they were all clustered round me, presumably waiting for my reaction, but what with the intense heat and my growing hunger, I could only stare dumbly at them, and was considerably relieved when one of the aerodrome officials said: "If Madame would not mind, she could stay at my home. I am on night duty and have to meet the next plane at three o'clock in the morning. She can have my bed, as I will not need it."

Everybody thought this an excellent idea, so after dropping the other passengers at their various lodging houses, M. Maurice escorted me, not without pride, to his house. It was one in a row of minute white boxes, with a high wall round it and a pocket- hand-kerchief-sized square of cement for a garden. Inside, one room was divided into two by a screen, behind which was a handsome double bed, hung with a white lace canopy. M. Maurice put his head through a window and called: "Julie! Maria!" There was some giggling and scuffling, and two negresses appeared, followed by two very much lighter-coloured children, aged about two and three. They stared, entranced, at me, while he gave them orders to change the sheets on the bed and to bring me a drink. I began — in my very indifferent French — to thank him, but he brushed this aside with a wave of his hand. "All night I have to work, it will not incommode me at all." Then, with a courtly bow, he kissed my hand and left.

The two negro girls bustled about, while the children stood staring round-eyed, as I tore off my stifling sweater and wrapped my thin dressing-gown around me. I was shown to a little bath-place, with a huge jar of cool water and a dipper. By the time I was finished, the bed was ready, and I said goodnight to the girls and lay down. It was unbearably hot, and without a net, the mosquitoes were a nuisance. In self-defence, I wrapped myself in the top sheet like a corpse and lay, gently sweating, until I drifted into sleep.

I was awakened suddenly by feeling the bed move, and opening my eyes cautiously, saw that my host had lain down beside me, dressed — so far as I could see — only in his shirt. He lay perfectly still, and I rolled carefully to my edge of the bed, stepped on the floor, still wrapped in my sheet, and stole round the screen, where I sat down on an uncomfortable gilded "loveseat".

4

After a minute or two, the bed gave a protesting groan. There was a patter of footsteps, and round the screen came M. Maurice. I could see him clearly in the moonlight, his collarless white shirt above a pair of thin, hairy legs, and his bald head fringed with remarkable black hair. He threw himself on his knees on the floor beside me and tried to take my hand. This he found unable to do, as I still had them crossed over my chest in the manner of a corpse holding a winding sheet.

"Excusez-moi! Excusez-moi!" he faltered, gazing wildly into my eyes with an expression of exaggerated despair. It was almost impossible to avoid exploding with laughter. Not daring to look him in the face, I got to my feet and paced majestically up and down the room, my spare piece of sheet trailing with a faint swishing sound on the floor behind me. He trotted along after me, apologies streaming from his lips. He had not meant to insult me, he was so tired and had only intended to lie down for half an hour, he knew I came from a good family. In this ridiculous procession, we swept round and round the tiny room until I could control my inward laughter, then I sat down and with a queenly gesture of my hand stopped him. "I quite understand," I said, "working so hard, you must be exhausted, but I am not accustomed to sharing my bed with strangers."

Laughter overcoming me at the sound of my own clumsy French, I shot to my feet, and we resumed our procession until finally I allowed myself to be persuaded to go back to bed, he having given me his sacred word of honour that he would not come within two metres of the screen. I could not sleep, however, as from the other end of the room came a steady stream of heart-broken sighs and groans, until about half an hour later he left the house.

Next morning, the two negresses woke me at seven o'clock, giving me a very hearty welcome. As I was having breakfast, M. Maurice arrived and joined me, but neither of us referred to the recent nocturnal drama. We did, however, discuss the chances of my getting a bed elsewhere, as my boat was not due for another two days, and just as I was saying goodbye, he seized my hand, knelt down beside my chair, and in a shaking voice, possibly intended to convey abject remorse, said: "Forgive me, forgive me. I know you are of good family, please dine with me tonight at the hotel."

I said I should be delighted, and wreathed in smiles, he departed for the airport. I tramped about in the burning heat for most of the day, until I found a bed as a paying guest in the house of a French family. By the time the boat arrived, I felt that I had really exhausted the amenities of Dakar.

The steerage passage to Brazil was uncomfortable but great fun, as most of the passengers were emigrating to Latin America and were in the highest spirits at having escaped the awful fate of being sent to Libya as colonists. Mussolini had forbidden all emigration to the Americas excepting for persons joining families already settled there who would undertake full responsibility for them, since they could take neither money nor valuables with them. On the other hand, if they went to North Africa, they were given every assistance and encouragement. It seemed North Africa was the last place they wanted to go to. There was also some risk that an Italian applying for a visa for South America might suddenly find himself en route for Tripoli. The voyage passed quickly enough, in an atmosphere overcharged with rejoicing, but I was glad to disembark.

Somewhere I read, or had been told, of the Falls of Iguacu, on the borders of Brazil and Argentina, and near Paraguay. They were supposed to be the third largest falls in the world. My magpie brain had stored away this bit of information, and I was determined to try and reach the falls as it might be my only chance of seeing tropical South America. I knew I could go from there to Buenos Aires, where I intended taking the train to cross the Andes for Valparaiso, Chile.

While planning my journey, I had found out that two boats left every summer from Valparaiso, bound for Punta Arenas in Patagonia. I decided that, if I wasted no time in cities, it should — with luck — only take a few days longer to reach Buenos Aires by way of Iguacu than by sea, but since I had no idea how to get to Iguacu, I decided to break a self-imposed rule and use one of my letters of introduction. This was a departure from principle, because I have always considered using this advantage to be an unfair method of seeking help, since the unfortunate recipient feels bound to offer it. I feel no qualms in accepting chance help, spontaneously offered, but presenting a letter of introduction is a form of blackmail.

Mr. Clark, head of a big import firm, however, appeared genuinely pleased to see someone fresh from Europe, although he was unable to answer my questions about Iguacu, or do more than promise to obtain all the necessary information while he took me to lunch. A clerk was already waiting with the details, when we returned from a splendid meal.

I had to go to Sao Paulo first, taking a train from there to a place called Presidente Epitacio, and on by various boats. He was not very sure about the route. The modern hotel had been burnt down two years before, due, he hinted darkly, to the Argentinians, who had a rival establishment just across the border, and no tourists had gone there, so that the travel agencies had lost interest. There would be no difficulty about getting on to Buenos Aires from the falls, as there was regular weekly service by boat.

That night, I took the train to Sao Paulo, cool on its high plateau, commercial, bustling and modern. The city itself did not appeal to me at all, so that I was glad to find I could leave the same night. I booked a second-class sleeper. On boarding the train, I found that I was sharing my compartment with the Lithuanian Consul, who was on his way back to the falls. It was a stroke of luck for me, as not only did he speak good Portuguese, but was able to speak with me in French. He was a small dapper man with a slightly Mongolian face and an unpronounceable name. He wore a white dust coat, which lent him a curiously clinical appearance. As nearly all the other passengers were wearing them, they were obviously the normal wear for Brazilian gentlemen on a journey to the Interior.

The train leaped and bounded away into the night. Leaping and bounding was a peculiarity of Brazilian trains, which gave the impression that the wheel and track were of slightly different measurements. The Consul entertained me with stories of people who had been thrown off trains altogether on their way to the restaurant car. However, we succeeded in making the journey safely, and had a perfectly disgusting meal of tapioca boiled in fish stock, followed by the corpse of the fish. I was only saved from starvation by what the Consul, with a sly laugh, called a "matrimonio". A slice of guava cheese on top of a slice of ordinary white cheese, a delicious combination that was (thank heaven) served everywhere, and constituted, in my limited experience, absolutely the only food worth eating in rural Brazil.

After a certain amount of palaver, I stowed myself away on the upper berth, and the Consul resigned himself to being alone on the lower.

In the morning, the Brazil of my imaginings was all round me. All, except for the neat coffee plantations, was a thick tangle of tropical green. Intermittently, the train stopped at a village that was trying to pass for a town with some elaborate name. There were very few passengers and three of them were army officers. By the time we reached Presidente Epitacio, which was just a collection of tumbledown huts, with no sign of a river, I was getting a little tired of the Consul. I was glad when the army officers approached me.

The stoutest, most senior and most scented, introduced himself as Colonel Branco, and his slightly thinner friend as Major da Silva. The third — a negro — who looked thin enough to be a mere lieutenant, was not introduced. They spoke in French, but with such a strong Brazilian accent, that I had some trouble getting used to it. A car drove up, and the Colonel invited me to drive down to the boat with them. I was gallantly handed in, followed by the Colonel, who, catching his tight breeches on a nail, sat down with an explosive noise, as the material ripped from buttock to waist. I gave a quick look to ascertain whether it was to be a laughing matter, but the Major and the negro were as solemn as owls.

A little way along a dusty road we came to the Parana, a broad, red, unwatery-looking river that made a strange sucking noise as it flowed past. Tied to a rickety jetty was a paddle steamer, very small and shabby, but flying an enormous Brazilian flag. The sight of my first gaucho — a motionless figure on a horse, wrapped in a scarlet poncho, a huge black sombrero on his head, watching some miserable-looking cows — lent the whole scene an air of romance. Carefully backing out of the car, the Colonel told the Major to escort me onto the boat, where I found, much to my relief, that I had a small, oven-like cabin to myself.

The boat was tiny, having only about four cabins, and the rest of the passengers were squatting about on deck, presenting a tremendous variety of shades in complexion, and clothes of almost every colour except white. Something about the Brazilian climate seems to dispel race-consciousness, and even the Japanese — most race-conscious of all peoples — have thrown themselves into the general melting-pot.

We churned downstream for a couple of hours, and then anchored for the night. At sunset, all the passengers assembled below the flag, and while the Colonel's beautifully manicured hands reverently lowered it, the Major conducted the singing of the national anthem, gracefully waving his hand to an imaginary band. A young girl of about 14 led a dissident group, in a considerably more nasal version, with quite a different rhythm. After a dinner even worse than that served by the railway, the Consul tried to explain to the Colonel the difference between an English miss and a señorita.

Next morning we steamed away at daybreak, stopping whenever the Captain saw a stick with a white rag tied to it stuck in the bank. This was a sign that a passenger was waiting. All were gauchos or their families. The gauchos startled me by bursting into tears when they said goodbye. They had no luggage, each just carried a saddle, but some women often had a parrot in a cage, or a monkey. The women wore long cotton dresses with full skirts, and rode side-saddle behind their men, or alone sitting sideways on a man's saddle, and seemed to be able to stay on whatever the pace. I could not find out what happened when they disembarked: did they buy horses, steal them or lasso wild ones? Unfortunately, no one could supply an answer to this enthralling question. At one landing stage, there were a few warehouses, and this was the port for Matto Grosso, 15 days riding away. Quite a few passengers went ashore with their saddles, but the only horses I could see had riders seated firmly on their backs.

The heat was oppressive when we left, and we all were lying sweating about the deck, when suddenly one of the sailors gave a shout. The Major leapt to his feet and fired about four times with his revolver into the river; it was a capybara, a kind of water pig. At the third shot it sank, but the boat chugged steadily on and such was the state to which Brazilian food had reduced me that my only feeling was one of bitter disappointment that we would not be having a change of diet. Towards evening, the boat stopped alongside a pleasant grassy bank, a gangplank was put out, and one of the crew ran along it and with a machete began to cut some steps in the bank. The steamer gave several shrill whistles. We had made Port Guaryre, and the boat could go no farther as the river here turns into seven waterfalls. Several cars arrived, mostly with military visitors, come to pay their respects to the Colonel. After the welcome was over, he gave me a lift in his car to the hotel, which turned out to be surprisingly good. Then we went for a quick look at the waterfalls, which were remarkable.

The next part of the trip was by courtesy of the Yerba Maté company, who practically owned Porto Mendez, the point at which the river becomes navigable again. They operated a narrow-gauge railway which took about two hours for the descent. The Colonel, still being very gallant, offered me a seat in the special car that had been procured for his use. Since this one was leaving after the regular one, he would have time to show me round the town. We had a slightly better dinner in the hotel, and then started our sightseeing. Unfortunately for the Colonel, the whole town consisted of just the area outside the hotel. A square illuminated by strong lights, flanked on one side by the railway, on the other by the hotel, with a background of a few houses. However, he made the most of it. The square had been divided by a net, and a game between the bachelors and married men was in progress. The Colonel said they were playing volley-ball and certainly the ball was the right size, but the players stood shoulder to shoulder, many more than usual, on each side of the net and pushed the ball back and forth, the side that let it drop to the ground being the loser. After we had studied the game, the Major pointed out the wooden shingles on the few houses, another object of interest, and was casting a despairing look round to see what else he could point out, when a soldier appeared, saluted, and announced that the car was ready to take us to the railway 300 yards away across the square. We all climbed solemnly in, the Colonel last, as Brazilian etiquette demands that as soon as the person of highest rank is seated in any conveyance, it must move off immediately.

The special train was enchanting — an open T-model Ford, painted bright scarlet, on four little wheels to fit the Lilliputian track, it was coupled to a toy locomotive, also painted scarlet. We piled in, and almost before the Colonel had sat down, it steamed off. There was a full moon, and as we rushed through the night, the Colonel asked me how I enjoyed travelling *"entre le maïs et l'immensité"*. Every now and then, small animals like rabbits ran across the line. As the Colonel had said, the immensity of the sky and endless fields of maize — raggedly purple-grey in the night — held a curious unreality, as we rushed along in the brightly painted toy train. I was sorry when the 68 kilometres were behind us and we pulled up by some big *maté* sheds housing a funicular that ran down a steep bank to the boat, a hundred feet below.

Next morning we got to Iguacu. The hotel was exactly like one in the old-fashioned cowboy films; only dancing girls in spangles were lacking. It was a two-storied wooden shack, with all the paint peeling off, and a ladder leading to the top floor, which was divided into cubicles by walls that stopped three feet short of the ceiling. The name painted on the outside was "Hotel Progresso". It was very full, but during my five days there, I never saw anyone do a stroke of work, and seldom saw anyone move at all, excepting for the Lithuanian Consul, who visited the falls with me. The rest of the inhabitants spent their time sleeping loudly, both afternoon and night, waking up now and then to go and have a shower. This in itself required some skill as, in this tropical heat, masses of boiling water gushed out of the cold tap and nothing at all from the hot.

The Consul and I went out early next morning to try to arrange our visit to the falls. We both spoke German, the Consul very well. Luckily, he had taken great pains to find out the best thing to do and had heard that Herr Harry Schinke, who owned the only motor vehicles in Iguacu, was the expert, but it was not always easy to get him to take you himself. Herr Harry, slight and fair, and married to a very pretty Brazilian girl, was, in contrast to everyone else, supercharged with energy. He promised to come for us in one of his cars next morning.

It was a relief to slip out early, from the stuffy hotel still droning with snores, into the dirty street made briefly attractive by the fresh dew. Harry came banging up in his best ramshackle car — the word "best" merely referring to the condition of the engine. We got in and he wired the door shut, and we chugged down a grass track, with thick jungle on either side. He stopped from time to time in front of a curtain of greenery, which Harry would demolish with a few strokes of his machete, saying, "It grows up quickly in two weeks." We passed abruptly out of the jungle, and in front of us was a great plain strewn with rocks and patches of water. As soon as the engine stopped, we could hear the gurgling of the water, rushing towards the falls, which plunged over the huge, horseshoe-shaped curve of the cliff dropping in front of us.

Harry got out and started stowing the food under the car. "Why under the car?" I asked, thinking of ants. "Otherwise wild horses will eat it," he said. "They are cunning devils." He looked proudly round. "It is lovely here, but wait till I've taken you down. That will thrill you." It was plain that he regarded the falls as his own. He led the way to a small track he himself had made, and we started down. It was steep, twisted and soaking. At some places Harry made us rope up, at others he had put in rickety ladders. It was fascinating dodging about behind the tremendous rushing power, and we were wet, laughing and triumphant when we reached the bottom.

The falls drop in two long cascades, a shelf of roots jutting out halfway. Harry took us onto the rock shelf behind the waterfall, across to the other side, and then up to the top again, and back to the car over some giant stepping-stones. The sun shone fiercely, and we were dry in a few minutes and ready to go bathing in the pool that Harry showed us. While we swam about, Harry cut some fresh green branches and started a smoky fire. He retrieved the sandwiches from under the car and laid them out invitingly in the smokiest area. Protesting and coughing, I grabbed mine and went to the other side, but he called: "Come back! The insects will devour you away from the smoke." I looked at my arms and legs. They were already covered with a greyish cloud of the smallest gnats I have ever seen. I hurried back into the water and sat there immersed to the chin. Harry himself seemed quite impervious. "For six months when I first came I was swollen all over from the bites, but now I don't taste good any more," he told me.

The rest of the day we spent protecting ourselves against the insects by water and smoke, putting off as long as possible the return to the horrors of the Hotel Progresso, and it was dark by the time we finally returned. The next three days after seeing the falls were appalling. The rest of the guests in the hotel were men of various colours and they spent their entire day in pyjamas, which I suppose was practical, as sleep was their only pastime. The Colonel and the Major filled me with amazement. They seemed to be able to maintain their sole interest — sex — on a diet of small black beans in a sticky gunmetal-coloured sauce. On me the effect of the beans was quite different; when finally I was driven by hunger to eat them, they only gave me wind. It was Harry Schinke who really saved my reason. He got a horse for me to ride, showed me the best place for bathing and then sent his young sons to stone iguanas and invited me to his house to eat them. His pretty Brazilian wife cooked them and they were delicious. They had lovely tender white meat that tasted a little like frogs' legs and was far more satisfying.

The day the boat was due from Argentina, I was listening as keenly as the townspeople for the sound of a cannon. This was the big weekly event, for it announced the cinema. "If the ship brings the film, the cinema will open at six o'clock, so listen for the cannon which will fire twice, if the film arrives," said the notices on the walls. The cannon did fire twice.

That evening the Colonel, the Major and the Consul invited me to go with them to see the film, which was about 20 years old, jerky and scratched, and it was obviously the least important part of the evening. The cinema really being an excuse for the younger people to avoid chaperones, they sat close to each other and dallied in the darkness. Smoking was forbidden except for the operator.

In spite of Harry's care, I only just managed to make the boat on my own two feet, my legs being a pair of thick, repulsive-looking columns. The boat itself was a joy, with proper cabins and clean sheets, a bathroom, dining room, and a miraculous steward, who after taking one look at my legs, disappeared, and returned with a pot of balm, which, he promised me with perfect truth, would reduce them to normal size in two days. Thus cossetted, the short journey to Posadas in Argentina passed like a flash. The best things were the food and watching the shore of Paraguay, which while looking much the same as Argentina, seemed to be inhabited by much more romantic figures. The Paraguayans are the most quixotic of the South Americans, the men spending most of their lives fighting for their country or their honour. As a result, only about one man in seven survives long enough to get married, but then he can marry up to seven wives, so that no Paraguayan woman need fear spinsterhood.

CHAPTER TWO
CHILEAN HOSPITALITY

B Y the time we reached Posadas, my legs had quite recovered, so I walked to see the ruins of a town that had once been the small independency called Missiones, run by Jesuit Fathers for the benefit of the Indians. It had been modelled on the lines of the Inca civilization. A place for everybody and everybody in his place.

It had been a thriving community, completely self-contained and self-supporting, with a very high standard of living, but without freedom. About a hundred years ago, the Argentine Government had protested to the Pope against this independent enclave inside their territory, and, by order of the Vatican, the Fathers were obliged to leave.

The Indians sank quickly back into a state of primitive squalor. As I walked round the roofless, overgrown ruins, in which the descendants of the original Indians now camped, it was not very difficult to visualise how it must have once looked. I wondered if these present-day Indians were happier now than their forebears had been under the Jesuits. Herds of emaciated cattle, covered with sores, surprised me, not being at all what I was expecting from Argentine beef, but it did explain the toughness of all the meat I had eaten so far. Later on I found out that these were the cattle that were made into corned beef.

Now that the river was bigger, we transferred to a larger steamer, but still only had three passengers on board as we went down to Corrientes, headquarters of the Swiss-run Yerba Maté Company. Here I met Henri Berger, a Swiss employed by the

14

company. He showed me round the sheds where the *mate* was lying bagged for shipment to the south, and told me that the word "*mate*" did not mean the leaf, but was the name of the gourd from which the *yerba*, or leaf, is drunk.

He then drove me out to see the estate, and the houses in which the Swiss personnel lived. After the Hotel Progresso, they looked like palaces to me. I think he noticed I was a little disappointed to see that all signs of frontier life had gone, as he kindly asked me if I would like to shake hands with a man who had killed 50 men in duels. We drove back to the town and went to a cafe, where he hailed a large, jolly-looking man, dressed in loose trousers tucked into riding boots and a red cummerbund, with a shock of grey hair under a small beret. He introduced me, saying, "Señor Cardoza, Miss Boxer is very interested to meet you, because I told her that you had killed 50 men."

Señor Cardoza bowed deeply over my hand, murmuring deprecatingly, "It was nothing, nothing." As he seemed so pleased to be the object of this macabre attention, I asked him outright if he had really killed 50 men, and if there were no penalties attached. A big smile spread over his face.

"In Paraguay where I lived," he said, "they do not mind so much, because it is always in a fair fight, but when I shot my 50th man, I had to leave. Even in Paraguay they said 50 is too many." He sat down and had a drink with us, and I was quite miserable when I heard the steamer whistle to announce its departure.

On board everything was transformed. The ship was now crowded with passengers, and most of them were German. I was glad, as my German was so much better than my Spanish, and by the time we reached Buenos Aires, I had almost forgotten that I was in a Spanish-speaking country. The hotel I went to in Buenos Aires on their recommendation was called the Vierjahreszeiten. It was entirely staffed and run by Germans, having a big bierstube in the basement, where girls in Bavarian dress served drinks. As the evening wore on everyone sang lieder, with tears streaming down their faces. After one night of this I was so sickened by their sentimentality that I was thankful to be invited to lunch at the Jockey Club by the English manager of the big *frigorifico*. The Club, with all its coloured marble walls, pillars and stairs, reminded me of the Moscow underground. I caused some consternation by asking if I could have a tender steak, as in my ten days in Argentina, eating

15

meat twice a day, I had not yet had one tender piece. This put the head waiter on his mettle. "Please, Madam," he said, "wait a little and I promise you the best steak you will ever eat in your life." He was as good as his word. After 20 minutes a splendid, two-inch-thick grilled steak was laid before me. It was so tender that I had only to rest my knife on it, and with a gentle pressure cut right through. It was a dream steak, and I have never had another to touch it.

Next day I left by train for Santiago di Chile, where I was going to spend a few days with friends of my cousin. The train journey was depressing, as Argentina was suffering from a bad drought. As the train ran across the endless pampas, I got my first sight of what later I came to regard as part of the normal landscape: clean, picked bones of animals lying strewn about the ground. Now it was worse than usual. As the train rumbled along we passed the idle windmills that should pump up water into the iron troughs. Windmills and troughs were still there, but not a drop of water, and round each trough stood the shrunken, dying cattle, some already collapsed, others dead and stinking, and strewn about them piles of clean, picked bones. This was a constantly recurring scene, and by the time the train got to Mendoza, I was worn out with emotion. Mendoza itself was almost another shock, with streams of fresh water, lovely fruit and luscious greenery.

Crossing the Andes is a wonderful way to come to Chile. As soon as the train wound its way from the snowy heights, I knew I was in another country. Landscape, flowers, trees, everything seemed different, and with the sudden rush down the mountainside, the climate appeared to change six months in as many hours. Santiago was filled with flowers, and the welcome I got from people who had never seen me before made it feel like entering Paradise.

The Browns belonged to one of the English families that had settled in Chile and were entirely bilingual in Spanish and English. Their Chilean surroundings had lent them a kind of natural, careless gaiety that was captivating. They were amused by, but tolerant of, my earnest enquiries as to when the first boat would be leaving for Magallenes.

"It is meant to leave in two days time, but of course it won't as there is sure to be a strike. Anyway, you could always catch it in the south, at Puerto Monte, and spend Christmas with us...."

"But how do you know that there will be a strike?" I asked.

"Because every year there is a strike. Only two boats go down to Punta Arenas each year for the wool clip, and they must go in summer and get back before the bad weather. The crews strike each year, just before the boats sail, and after a week's delay, they get a rise and off they go."

However, the first thing next morning, I was down at the shipping office to find out the earliest sailing date, only to be told: "I am sorry, but we do not know because there is a strike. The boat will be delayed for at least four days."

The Browns laughed when I told them, and said, "That's fine. Now you really will be able to spend Christmas with us." So three days later I left by train for Valparaiso to catch the boat if it sailed, or spend New Year's Eve with friends I had made in Santiago if it did not. Chilean hospitality is astounding. Once I had stayed with one family it was as though I had a passport into every Chilean home, and I began to feel rather rude with my tiresome refrain of "When will the boat leave for Magallanes?"

In Valparaiso there was the same answer to my question: the strike was still on and nobody knew when it would end. The only thing that I managed to find out was that the boat could not possibly leave Puerto Monte before January 14th. Puerto Monte was the last port-of-call before the Patagonian Channels, and terminus of the railway.

Following my invitations south, I decided to see as much of the countryside as I could. So I found myself on the train to Valdivia, where I was going to stay on the farm of a Mr. Mitchell. Valdivia was a completely German community, several of the shops going so far as to have notices saying *"Habla Espanol"* in their windows. The town was in a fever of excitement as the Germans were sending out a battleship on a goodwill tour, and the settlers had organised the whole town for their reception. Each house and farm was allotted its quota of officers and men, all strictly graded according to rank: the most senior officers on the largest farms, while the sailors were mostly billetted in the town. Mr. Mitchell was quite disgusted with it all.

I had arrived in time for the harvest; each farm had its own threshing, which was called a *"trecia"*. Mr. Mitchell's had just finished, but he took me to see his neighbour's. As we rode across the fields we could easily see where it was taking place. Groups of horsemen were riding in from every direction. Men with their wives riding pillion behind them, or women riding side-saddle in their full cotton dresses with a couple of children up behind. The mares ran ahead. Females in Chile do fairly well: even though they may be considered foolish and are on no terms of equality with men, at least they are not expected to do much work either. This principle is carried into the animal world, mares never being ridden.

The wheat was piled high on a flat circular area of trampled earth, inside a high wooden fence. Three men with pitchforks were perched on top of the mound of wheat; outside the fence stood the rest of the neighbours, armed with long staves. With shouts and blows the mares were driven into the enclosure, two mounted men behind them. While the men on the mound pitchforked the wheat under the mares' hooves, the mounted ones drove them round the circle. Outside the fence, the people also urged them on by shouting and, if they showed any signs of slowing down, hitting them with the staves. This went on all day, until the wheat was threshed, with intervals for reversing the mares as they became giddy. The men worked in shifts which got shorter as the day got hotter and the wine began to take effect.

A *trecia* is a kind of working fiesta. The neighbours loan their mares and labour, and the farmer provides the food and the wine — the wine being by far the most important item. While the threshing was going on, the women lit fires outside and cooked a dismal dish called "*puchero*", a watery stew of meat and vegetables with all the flavour boiled out. By the time it was ready, the threshing was nearly done and most of the men so filled with wine that they would not know what they were eating. As coffee was being served, we heard the sound of a guitar and saw a crowd gathering.

"Come and see them dance," said Mr. Mitchell. We edged our way into the circle forming round the dancers. The man, his hands gripping each other firmly behind his back, his body bent forwards, fixed his eyes gloatingly on the woman's face, leaping furiously round her, while she held her eyes modestly down, twisting a clean handkerchief between her hands, as she keeps turning to face him, and alternately encouraging and repulsing him. We did not stay very long. By this time hardly anyone was sober and arguments were beginning.

"We had better be moving before any real trouble starts," Mr. Mitchell said.

"Is there always trouble?" I asked.

"Well, I've lived here all my life, and I have never known a *trecia* without a knife fight and someone getting wounded, and quite often killed."

As we rode back, he was very cheering about my trip to Patagonia. "Lots of nonsense is talked about how dangerous this country is for women," he said, "but these men have all been conditioned by the Spanish tradition of courtesy towards ladies, and provided you behave yourself properly and the men do not get a chance to get drunk, you will be far safer here than in London or New York."

"Well, I would like to try a short ride here, if I could," I said. "There are those three lakes — Calafquen, Panguipulli and Rinichui. Do you think I could go to them and still get down to Puerto Monte by January 14th?"

"Well, you can try," he laughed. "I can start you off from here with a couple of horses and a *huazo*. He will go with you to the hotel at Panguipulli. Then you could probably muddle on from there. There is nearly always some way of getting round, and it would be wonderful practice for you."

Early next morning, the *huazo* and I started off. I felt a romantic figure as I was wearing the Chilean version of a poncho, called a *"manta castilla"*, made of shiny black wool with long hairs sticking out. It was absolutely waterproof and much bigger than the ponchos of the northern parts of South America, covering a large part of the horse as well as its rider. The day was lovely, clear and fresh, the snow-capped Cordillera glittered along the horizon. Best of all was the fact that at last I was riding in a part of the world where riding was the only form of transport. I had always wanted to journey on horseback, but could not enjoy riding as a means of travel in places where cars or buses were the normal thing. Here in Chile and the Argentine I felt I was still just in time to discover a few places not yet opened up to motor transport.

We went along at a jog-trot, which at first I found hideously uncomfortable and thought that my teeth would be shaken out. By watching the *huazo* carefully and making myself forget all I had ever learnt about rising to the trot and pulling on the reins to guide the horse, I managed at last to relax enough to enjoy myself. I got to prefer this way of riding. There was much more harmony between horse and rider: the horse was expected to do his own thinking. To change direction, I learnt to lay the reins across the horse's neck and shift my weight onto the side to which I wanted to turn, and I never had trouble once I managed to mount. This was always my biggest difficulty, riding as I did, horses mostly belonging to *huazo*s or gauchos who are inveterate show-offs. There was nothing they liked better than to be seen leaping on a prancing horse which, once mounted, would give a couple of bucks.

The track appeared a little hard to follow, not that this bothered me, as I was pinning my faith on the *huazo*, although he seemed to be undeserving of such trust, and we must have made a detour to each little squatter's house between Mr. Mitchell's and the hotel. I may be maligning him, of course; it could have been natural courtesy that took us from house to house. In remote areas away from the road, and without radios, the only means of getting news is from passing travellers. The four leagues which should have taken a couple of hours, took nearer five, but there was still the whole afternoon for me to make enquiries about how to get on. The *huazo* was going with me to Lake Calafquen in the morning. After that he would take the horses back to Mr. Mitchell.

The hotel in Panguipulli was small and simple with only two other guests. Lunch was over when we got there, so I got out my Spanish phrase book and launched upon my enquiries as to how to get to Lake Rinichui. Local opinion, for by the time I had made myself understood even the carabineers had arrived on the scene to help, was unanimous. Horses would be impossible, but there was a launch, and it might go, although just where it was bound for I could not make out. Certainly not for the only place name that I knew. However, they all seemed to think that the "launcha" was the thing for me, and one of the carabineers offered to take me to see the mechanic. Still clutching my dictionary, I followed him down to the lakeside, where a shabby launch was moored. A man was lying on the deck, a bottle of wine beside him.

He jumped up when the carabineer shouted, extending a black greasy hand for me to shake. He and the carabineer held a rapid conversation, while I tried to butt in every now and then, feverishly searching the dictionary as soon as I recognised a word. There was something about a delay, but after that I may have misunderstood the drift of the talk, because I worked it out as referring to a corpse. However, in the end it looked as if we had succeeded, and I understood that if the launch left it would go the following afternoon and I could go with it.

Absolutely exhausted by all the brain work, I tottered back to the hotel to find dinner had already started. The other guests were on their fruit course, but my place was easily distinguished by the plates, with slowly congealing food of the preceding courses arrayed round it. Breakfast was an affair of exact timing, too, as I found when I asked for breakfast at six o'clock, only to be told that it was served at eight o'clock, not before and not after.

The *huazo* and I rode off breakfastless next morning to see Lake Calafquen. It was a perfect day, and the ride alone would have been well worthwhile even if there had been no lake at the end of it. Two volcanoes towered above, and part of the route ran beside a glass-clear river connecting the two lakes. Best of all, we suddenly came across a group of Araucanian Indians. They belong to the one tribe that has never been conquered and have survived up to the present day, depleted but fiercely independent. They were a fine-looking group, the women noble and attractive with their heavy silver jewellery. It wasn't until we had left them some way behind us that I realised what had drawn my attention to them in the first place. They were not riding, and I saw no signs of horses.

When we got back to the hotel, lunch was so thoroughly over that they had not even left my food round my place, so I crept into the kitchen with the *huazo* and persuaded them to give us some *"harina tostada"*. This is a Chilean standby made of roasted and ground wheat kernels, which can be eaten hot or cold, with milk or water, and lasts indefinitely if kept dry. While I was gobbling this down, I heard a steam whistle and a child came running in to say that the "launcha" was leaving.

Although it was the siesta hour, the passengers were ready and when the mechanic saw the hotel contingent, he urged his horn to a piercing shriek. We all rushed up the gangway, then waited in dead silence for about 20 minutes. At last from the carabineer's house, ten figures staggered out, each grasping a wine bottle. Arriving opposite the launch, they all offered each other a last swig from their ten bottles. Then they lowered their two drunkest members into a rowing boat loaded down with cases of *maté*. A bottle of wine was put on a case between them, and after a few pulls at it, they both became unconscious, and the rowboat was tied to the stern of the launch.

The rest, one of whom turned out to be a girl with two front teeth missing and dressed in trousers and a man's hat, began saying goodbye. After some shuffling and pushing, three stayed behind and the rest, including the girl, came on board. The mechanic wound up his horn again and, as its piercing wail died down slowly, we chugged quietly away. He then put a small boy in charge of the steering and turned his attention to the girl, who responded ardently. The man who up to now I had taken for her husband had fallen asleep, and stepping round him they retreated into a hutch-like cabin and hung a poncho across the entrance.

After about a couple of hours of erratic dashes across the lake, as the child steersman followed the advice of various passengers, we stopped to let a man off. He first came up to me, bowed and said in fair English, "My wife is English. She would like you to come to tea with her."

"What about the launch?" I asked, but the mechanic, keen to get back to his love, said he could wait.

Although we could see the house a few hundred yards away, horses were waiting on the landing stage. As we came towards the house, I saw that the wire enclosure surrounding it was thickly crowded with hens. They all ran squawking round the door as it opened and followed the wife as she came down to the gate to meet us.

"I can see you are English," she said. "We are ready for tea. Please come in and join us."

She was from Devonshire, and I have no idea how or where she met her husband. They had seven children, the eldest a boy of 18, the youngest a child of six. The house was tiny, having only two rooms.

"We have only been here two years, and there is always so much to do," she said. "Oh, how nice of you to come; if only we had more room you could have stayed with us."

The tea was unforgettable. Ten of us sat round a table loaded with plates of hot scones, huge bowls of Devonshire cream, and dishes of their own honey. It was obvious that they had very little money, but with such good food in abundance, the children all looked like cornflake advertisements. A sudden shriek from the launch horn interrupted us, and I rode back to the boat to find that we had a new passenger whose arrival had made quite a transformation in the crew. The mechanic had abandoned the girl and put on a clean shirt and a hat and was standing beside the steering wheel giving orders to the boy, who was casting off the lines.

As we left, the stranger came up and asked if I spoke French. He introduced himself as Pedro Gonzalez and said he was going to the next stop where the owner of the launch lived and was to stay with him for a few days of fishing. After about half an hour we came alongside a little jetty, where the rancher was waiting with some horses, and no sooner were we introduced than he invited me to stay too.

"My wife is the only woman here, and she would love to have company," he said, adding, "there is the house, take this horse and go on up. Tell her I have invited you to stay; she speaks French too."

Here again was this charming Chilean hospitality that gives the feeling of being carried along by a warm, fast-flowing river. I mounted and jogged up to the house. It was built of logs and had an enormous chimney out of which came a thin plume of smoke. It was growing dusk, and when I walked in I found it hard to see. The room looked huge, with a great fireplace at the far end. As my eyes got accustomed to the dim light, I could see a woman's figure bending over the hearth, arranging the logs. She straightened up and turned round as she heard my footsteps, and I was startled by her beauty. Her hair was magnificent, a rich shining chestnut that caught the light from the fire and from the oil lamp as she lit it.

"Welcome," she said. "I hope you have come to stay. My name is Nicole."

There was a low stool by the fire, and I sat down on it. From it I could look up the big chimney, and there, hanging by their tails, were four large fish. Nicole smiled when she saw me looking at them.

"We catch them easily in the lake," she said. "*Tres facile.*" They looked to me rather large for trout, one of them must have weighed at least twelve pounds, but they were her fish, and her lake, so she should have known. Raymond, Nicole's husband, and Pedro now joined us. We sat around the fire drinking good Chilean Pisco and helping ourselves to snacks of smoked trout, later to be exchanged for wine and grilled meat. It was a lovely easy atmosphere, like the kind of life I always longed to live, in magnificent surroundings, shooting and fishing enough for food but no more. Living in a house built from the trees off my land and furnished by my own carpentry.

By the end of the evening, I discovered that this was not really the kind of life Raymond and Nicole actually lived. Raymond was a well-to-do businessman, and this house was his hobby. They just came to stay for holidays. The handmade furniture and the house, though made from trees off the place, was the work of skilled carpenters.

Next morning we rode out to the forest to see the logging, and then down to the lake by the sawmill where the rafts, or *balsas* as they were called, were being made up. We went down to the water's edge to look at them. They were square, ungainly things, made out of bundles of plank, cut ready for export. About five of the bundles lashed together formed a raft. An enormous oar was fixed at each end for manoeuvring in the rapids, and sticking up in the middle was a cleft stick to hold food and clothes out of danger when the water swept over the rafts.

Raymond offered me a horse to take me down to below the rapids, where I could catch a boat. The boat would take me to the road where, with luck, I would find a bus called, surprisingly, a "*gondola*", which would take me to the railway. But now, standing by the fast-flowing river and watching the *balsas* being made up, I decided that it was by *balsa* that I wanted to go, and as I followed the unsuspecting Raymond down to talk to the raftsmen, I was planning how I could get him to let me go on one.

"When will they be leaving?" I asked.

"I am not sure, but soon. This lot is nearly ready."

Working on the rafts was a picturesque set of sturdy men. "These are the men who run the rapids," Raymond told me. "It is a dangerous job. So many get drowned each year that they like to see for themselves that the rafts are properly made up before they start." My spirits fell a bit at this, but Raymond interrupted my line of thought to introduce me to one of the men.

"This is Juan. He is one of the best men. He has been running for several seasons."

Juan nodded gravely. "It is Santa Catarina who has protected me," he said, crossing himself reverently.

They then started a discussion on accidents. One man had recently been drowned when his raft had broken up going through the rapids. That gave me an idea.

"Do they swim?" I asked.

"Oh no, not one of them can swim," said Raymond cheerfully.

Since I always prided myself on my swimming, this news partly restored my confidence, and when I learned that they would be leaving the next day or the day after, my mind was quite made up. If only I could get Raymond to help me. The raftsmen would certainly never take me unless he told them to. I thought it would be best to wait till a good dinner and plenty of wine had worked its magic before asking him.

That evening poor Raymond was relaxing after a wonderful meal when I asked him if he thought the men would mind taking me on the raft. At first he was upset, but Chileans hate refusing outright, so at last, after I had made myself out to be a kind of international swimming champion, Raymond said I could go but only if the rafts left in two days. This suited me; everything was delayed in Chile, and one day was not long to wait in such a lovely place. Raymond said he would probably need a day to persuade the men to take me. They would have to be willing, otherwise if anything happened, they would blame him for making them take me. This was as much as I could hope for, so I went to bed quite content.

Next day, we all went down to the rafts again. After Raymond had spoken to the men, he brought them round to talk to me, and I shamelessly used my letter from *The Times*, telling them that I should be writing an account of this tremendous experience and that there would probably be pictures of the brave raftsmen in all the English papers. They were very taken with this prospect and said that I could certainly go with them.

Next morning we were all up early. Nicole, Raymond and Pedro came with me to the river. I took just my camera and a couple of smoked trout sandwiches, as Nicole had insisted that my luggage should go by pack-horse to the boat landing. At the sawmill we found two rafts ready and Juan eager to get started. For the first part of the trip to the head of the rapids there is only one man to each raft, and I boarded one with a man called Jose, Juan being on the raft behind us. The river was running fairly fast, and we swept away in tremendous style calling and waving goodbye. It did not seem to take very long to reach the rapids, and I could hear the torrent and see the spray as our raft was swung into the bank. Jose leapt ashore and secured it to a tree. As soon as he was back, Juan's raft came sweeping down and passed close enough for us to jump onto it. Jose rushed to the forward oar, just getting it into action as we hit the race. Waves burst right over us, coming up between the planks so that we were standing calf-deep in water. The two men, holding now this side, now that, to utilise the whole weight of their bodies, were quite safe from being swept off, but I had nothing to hang onto. Looking wildly round as I tried to keep my footing against the pull of the water, the only thing I could see above the water was the cleft stick with bundles of food tied to it. It did not appear to be anywhere nearly up to my weight, but, although it trembled, it stood firm. The men were laughing and shouting as they worked their oars waist-deep in white water, then suddenly the river widened and we were gliding along in calm water again.

As we went quietly down-river, they warned me that worse was to come, making quite sure that I understood by pantomiming us all lying dead in a row, our arms crossed on our chest, so as soon as I heard the roar of the next rapids, I gripped the cleft stick very firmly. There was a queer feeling of strength and insecurity about the raft. It was so large and firm, yet I could not accustom myself to the fact that it was apparently safer half-sunk. For me, the chief danger was to stop being dragged overboard by the tremendously powerful suction of the water up round my knees.

As soon as we reached the second rapids, I could see the danger the men had been trying to describe. The river entered a kind of gorge, and rocks stuck up everywhere: the water was white, like suds, clear across. About half-way down, two huge rocks showed plainly, with a smooth body of water passing between them. We too would have to pass between them, and the gap was only about a yard wider than the raft. Beyond the rocks was a two-foot drop. The spray was so thick and we rushed through with such speed that I had hardly time to be frightened before we were through to the next calm stretch. On this part, too, Juan and Jose regaled me with more details about deaths in the rapids, but my Spanish was too feeble to understand much more than the word "*muerte*", although, combined with the gesticulations, it was enough.

By the time we were shooting the third rapid, I was feeling such an old hand that I even managed to take a photograph, to the great delight of Juan and Jose. I was sorry to reach the lake and see the steamer tied to the jetty, but was keener than ever to get on to Patagonia. This little taste of Chilean travel, away from a road but comparatively civilised, made me long for a really long journey in a more sparsely populated and more primitive country.

There was no place to stay where the steamer was stopped, and I was wondering what to do when a young Chilean came up and spoke to me in German. His mother was German, married to a Chilean, and they ran a dairy farm. He invited me to stay the night with them and next morning got up at four a.m. so that we could ride as far as the bus to save me waiting for the steamer. By doing this I could catch an earlier train into Puerto Monte. When we got to the station, I asked what the date was and found that I was three days out and that the boat was due in Puerto Monte next day. At Puerto Monte, the boat against all reason was already there. She was small, shabby and painted grey. All the other passengers were already on board, not many, as there was so little accommodation. We sailed that evening.

The journey was bleak and freezingly cold. Bouts of driving rain swept down at least once a day, and sometimes all day. The view, whenever we caught a glimpse of it, was quite magnificent, but as we chugged in and out of the misty Patagonian Channels, there was a running refrain from my fellow passengers: "If only you could see this glacier/mountain/waterfall, you would say you had never seen anything lovelier."

The little boat was carrying only businessmen, two accompanied by their wives, and all with big interests in Patagonia. One of them was a Señor Braun who had been born in Punta Arenas. He did not look over 40, but from the tales of his childhood sounded as though he might have been 200. His father, in common as I was to find out later with all the older European inhabitants, had been a sailor who had jumped ship off the coast of Patagonia and had started a business buying and selling anything he could get hold of — mostly sealskins.

In the long winters, the whole family lived inside the warehouse, and Señor Braun's first recollections were of crawling about on the warehouse floor playing with gold coins, which had been the only currency and which his father kept in leather bags. Having no toys, the children had used the gold coins in all their games. Perhaps this was a good idea, for Señor Braun was now one of the richest men in Chile.

CHAPTER THREE
STARTING NORTH

P UNTA Arenas turned out to be a dreary modern town, swept by
a steady gale that whirled the dust up across the streets. Its
hotel, the Cosmos, had contrived to remain the same since the
day it was built, perhaps 30 years before, but as Patagonia itself
could only look back on 40 years of history, it ranked as an
ancient monument. Inside it was wonderfully comfortable, warm
and dry, with plenty of hot water, and perfectly delicious food,
afternoon tea being a regular feature. I was upset by an almost
total absence of horses, and cars swept up and down the tarmac
centre of the roads.

The town really lives, during summer, off the big mutton
freezers, butchers coming out yearly from England to take over
the slaughtering. I spent a most gruesome afternoon visiting one
at Rio Seco. We had to drive a few miles out to reach the huge
plant. A small jetty ran out from it into the sea, and there was a
boat tied alongside discharging live sheep from Tierra del Fuego.
We could see nothing but their hooves, as the sides of the jetty
were planked, but the air was filled with the sound of their trotting
feet, and beneath them the sea ran crimson from the blood of
those already killed. Inside the freezer, things were even more
horrible. We were given bundles of tripe to sniff, as they alone
smelled sweet, and saw the "Judas sheep" lead in each batch for
slaughter, then run past the butcher and slip out through an
escape hatch, while the butcher seized the following sheep and
rapidly cut its throat. Indeed, the manager was very proud of the

28

speed with which a live sheep was converted into a carcass in the freezer. It was something like two minutes, but I was not interested. I had quite decided to become a vegetarian, and I kept my resolution right up to the moment I saw a roast saddle of mutton in the Cosmos dining-room that evening.

A visit to the silver-fox farm was much more pleasant. Here the owners were up against much more entertaining problems: for instance, how to induce the male fox to accept more wives and how to keep white foxes white all year by making them pass the summer months surrounded by glaring white paint instead of snow.

But I was now growing anxious to be off and had already discovered that if I really wanted to stay in regions where riding was the only form of transport, I should have to remain among the foothill-pampas, which meant that I should explore only the edge of Patagonia proper.

I had been invited to stay at a ranch in the Ultima Esperanza district, run for a big company by a Mr. Baker. Like most company ranches, it proved very comfortable, with good heating, well-fitting doors and windows, and a lovely vegetable garden, protected by a windbreak of willows. As it was summer, there was quite a lot of coming and going. Now that there were roads and cars, people were able to visit each other without being forced to take a couple of days off, but it sounded from their conversation that many felt they had lost more than they gained. Patagonia came into being so recently, and had developed so fast, that the original pioneers were mostly still alive to enjoy the fruits of their labours, and their past hardships now appeared to them in a rosy light. When they heard what I wanted to do, they were full of solicitude. "Can you ride 50 miles a day on *maté* only?" they asked me, anxiously. "You must be careful there, as there are so few women. You should take a gun to defend yourself", and so forth. I found out that the last statement at least was quite unfounded, most Patagonians being staid family men, with anything between eight and 17 children. One thing upon which all were agreed was that I must meet the Masters family, on Lago Argentina, and also Mr. Lucas Bridges, north of Lago Viedma.

The route north that I wished to follow ran along the Chilean-Argentine border. It was closed during the summer in order to prevent the Argentinians from driving their sheep to the Chilean freezers. Mr. Baker took me to see the Argentine police to get permission to cross the border.

"You never quite know what these chaps will do," he said, "but you shouldn't have too much trouble. I won't talk, because they will be much more suspicious of me than of you."

We rode for about an hour before reaching the little police-shanty, in which two men in uniform were sitting, gazing into space. At the sight of visitors, they hurriedly buttoned up their tunics and smoothed down their hair. Mr. Baker introduced me and we embarked upon an elaborate exchange of courtesies, which I won hands down by replying to their compliments upon my courage by saying that, as men in Argentina were all true "*caballeros*", there could be no call for courage. They gave me permission to cross the border, and then, turning to Mr. Baker, assured him that should I get lost, he must inform them and they would personally go out and find me, cost them what it might.

Of course, I had to go and see the mylodon, or what remained of it. The gaucho who had found it now lived beside the little cave, and he showed me a couple of bones and a piece of hide on the shelf where he had found it. They looked to me as though they could have belonged to any Patagonian cow. As it was in fact a prehistoric cow, this need not have surprised me, but it was the state of preservation that was remarkable. I am always at a loss when confronted with this sort of thing. My imagination does not seem to function properly, and the guardian-gaucho, behaving like a high-priest handling the relics, struck me as slightly ridiculous.

I was greatly relieved when the conversation turned to the Hidden People of the Cordillera. The man who found the skin was, of course, a firm believer. They lived above the lakes, to the north (so he said), and the proof of their survival was that during certain years they would divert their water supplies and flood the lakes, doing enormous damage. All the attention he had attracted by being the finder of the mylodon might have accounted for his belief in the Hidden People, on such scanty evidence.

Now at last the day broke when I could start on my ride, but, unfortunately, a good month later than I had planned. It was now the first week in February. Mr. Baker had started me off with one of his gauchos. He had insisted on lending me an Australian army saddle, as he said I should never be able to manage on one of the

Chilean variety — usually just a couple of wooden cross-bars, with some sheepskins over them.

"How shall I get the saddle back to you?" I asked.

"Oh, no trouble at all, just give it to any gaucho coming this way and say it belongs to me," was his casual reply.

My first objective was the Masters' farm, but the whole project was very nebulous. I did not know the Masters, possessed the barest minimum of Spanish, and was to have the use of Baker's horse and gaucho for one day only, after which I had not the slightest idea how I would continue on my way. But I had absorbed the fact that, in such a scattered community, for total strangers to arrive and be warmly welcome (partly for the news that they bring with them from the outside world) is the normal thing.

Early next morning, Carlos and I, with two dogs and two horses, took the trail. Mr. Baker looked quite envious. "You will only just have time to see some parts of the country before they are tamed," he said, throwing a disdainful glance at the beautifully ordered place he ran. "I only wish that I had time to do the same. Don't worry about anything. It always works out all right in the end down here."

It was the best advice I have ever had, and I only wish I could always succeed in following it.

Carlos was evidently quite entertained at the idea of taking a "*gringa*", and was keen for me to admire his two sheep-dogs, which were small, rather like border collies, very tidy-minded and great respecters of property. So long as we were on Mr. Baker's land, the sight of straying sheep drove them to distraction, and they could not rest until these were organised into sizeable "points", as a small group of sheep is called. Any hares they put up under their noses were totally ignored. Carlos kept pointing out how efficient they were, but he never seemed to give them an order. How they knew that they had crossed the boundary onto the next farmlands, I could not discover, but when I noticed that they had passed two or three isolated sheep without taking any action, I asked if they were tired. He was deeply shocked. "Very good dogs," he said. "They always work, but this is not our land."

We did not meet a soul, and the scenery was bleak and grand, our route passing under some mountains called Baguales. No matter how near we came to their slopes, nor whether it rained or the sun shone, they were always glowering dark and remote. We rode for nine hours across barren land strewn with bones. The grazing looked so sparse that I thought the bones must be those of sheep that had died during the winter, when the mortality rate from severe storms is very high. The mortality in summer is fairly high too, but not from starvation. Indeed, the complaint when they arrive at the freezers is often that they are too fat. Above us, the condors swayed and floated, enormous scavenging birds that live in the Andes. They glide about, using the perpetual wind, never flapping their wings, ever searching for something large and dead, or small and helpless, for they are not courageous, although in the air they are lovely to watch. The wind, the bones and the condors were all so different from anything in my experience, that I felt as though I were on another planet.

Feathery white clouds occasionally swept across the huge, pale-blue sky. The bare earth was dotted with very sparse stunted shrubs, so desiccated that their roots seemed scarcely to penetrate the dry crust we rode over. Yet the horses seemed able to keep their jog-trot endlessly, and when, after eight hours, we reached a tiny shanty, I was horrified to see a telephone wire leading away from it, and to realise that civilisation is the hardest to escape from.

It was a tiny place used only in summer, but a pretty young Scots girl with five small boys — a shepherd's wife — was living in it. It was clean and tidy, and she gave us tea while controlling her young brood in a masterly fashion.

We then rode on to the main house, and met Mr. McLeod, the enthusiastic young Scotsman in charge. He had come out as a boy and was evidently a man of resource. Having once seen a picture of some skis, he decided to make some himself. He cut down a small tree, cut planks shaped roughly like the picture, boiled them for twelve hours to get the curved tips, and then took off. He was now making his third pair, and although a bit on the broad side, they looked quite professional to me.

Carlos left me here and took the horses back to Ultima Esperanza, but Mr. McLeod arranged for me to go on the next morning to the ferry that crossed the Santa Cruz, with some gauchos taking this route. The Santa Cruz river runs out of Lago Argentina eastwards to the sea. The ferry crossing is called after Charlie Fuhr, the first man to make the crossing, who built himself a hut on the opposite bank. The shack, being nearly 40 years old, was regarded as an antique.

The gauchos were taciturn, elderly men, and we all rode in solemn silence until we reached the ferry, when they became unexpectedly friendly, urging me to go inside a small *boliche* and have a drink with them. I thought this sudden friendliness suspicious, so decided to make my way directly to the raft, having first handed over my horse to the *boliche* proprietor to send back to Mr. McLeod with the next passing gaucho.

The ferry was a large, cumbersome, wooden affair that was pulled across the river on a steel cable, and by the time it left, there was a crowd of horses, gauchos and a woman with five children. The two eldest boys were six or seven, two were toddlers and there was a three-month-old baby. All were on horseback. She invited me to spend the night with a friend of hers, who would also probably be able to lend me a horse to carry on towards the Masters' farm. The friend turned out to be living in Charlie Fuhr's old house, and although it was only 200 yards from the ferry landing, I could see that the mother and the two elder boys were deeply embarrassed to be seen in the company of a pedestrian.

There was a sheep's carcass hanging up outside the house, and inside, the kitchen was nicely papered with sheets of brown paper off parcels and packages, for this was also the store, in a small way. Beyond was a bedroom and a store-room. A married couple lived there, with two small children, and at seven that evening, nine of us sat down to a meal of fried meat and *tortas*, an appalling paste of flour and water, fried in mutton fat. By the time the meal was finished, we were 15 in all, and with each new arrival, the hostess went out and whipped another slice from the carcass.

Immediately after dinner, we all went to bed, the women and children in the bedroom, the men outside, and I was given a pile of skins in the store-room, under rafters tastefully festooned with tripes. Next morning, the woman with the five children and three horses started off for her home. The two elder boys were up early to catch and saddle the horses. They helped their mother up, and, as she was riding astride, spent quite a time ingeniously covering her legs with a guanaco-skin cape. When she was settled with the baby, the two little boys mounted their horses, each taking a smaller child up onto the saddle behind them, and then they all moved confidently off on their 20-mile ride home, and I was left to try and find out how to make my way farther.

As I now found myself at the eastern edge of Lago Argentina, and as the Masters lived at the extreme northwestern end, I should have to follow the whole length of the lake. My hosts, being uncertain what to do with me, simply plied me with food. It is a kind of universal panacea in Patagonia. "When in doubt, eat!" seems to be the motto. Their major worry was that the wind would be too much for me, and, at half-hour intervals, they proffered food in some form. At last I persuaded them that if they could only lend me a really reliable horse, I should be perfectly capable of accomplishing the next stage, described as six leagues, by myself.

Here, for the first time, I came up against what turned out to be my major difficulty with the Spanish language. The favourite expressions were *"Como no?"* meaning "Why not?", and *"Quien sabe!"* or "Who knows!" An almost indefinite conversation can be carried on — all day, if need be. "Can I hire a horse, please?" *"Como no?"* It usually meant that the speaker was at least interested and prepared to try. But as it was my first experience, I began to get terribly upset, and the constant offerings of pieces of roast meat did not really help matters.

The animal they finally produced must have been one that had belonged to the late Charlie Fuhr. His whole head was grey with age, and only by kicking and much shouting could I get him to break into a reluctant lope. I felt I could not lose my temper with him, as he stood so patiently while I clambered on and off to open fences, yet by the time we had done six leagues, I felt as if I had done at least 12.

The country was beautiful. There is a chain of lakes going south, down the Cordillera, draining the big glaciers, and farther south their colour becomes ever more wonderful. I urged my ancient nag along the shore of the lake, my temper and frustration dying down rapidly. Such beauty as this I had never seen before. The extraordinary surface of the lake itself, like a great splash of duck-egg blue paint, seemed to retain its remarkable colour no matter whether the sun was hidden or shining. Snow-capped ranges to the west glittered sharply against the sky.

The farm I reached that evening was owned by a dear little German. He was most distressed at the idea of my riding to the

Masters. The proper way to go was by launch. The Masters had one, and as soon as there was not too much wind, they would send it out. All I had to do was to wait patiently for about five or six days until the wind, that never actually drops, should die down a little. Then would be the time to go.

Once again I found it much easier to deal with all these objections since I was able to talk German. He told me of another woman traveller, who had come through Patagonia a few years before, a German named Margret Geist. She had walked with an Alsatian dog from the snow-line in Alaska, and after seven years, had actually reached Punta Arenas. I was thankful to find out about her because, from now on, I could counter all objections to my journey on the score of safety by citing the example of Margret Geist.

Heinrich, my German host, had never been away from his farm. He was longing to ride with me to the next farm, but at the last moment his courage failed him. "Oh no," he cried, one foot in the stirrup, "I cannot do it. I have never been there, I do not like strange places." So I set off alone, turning every now and then to wave to the forlorn little figure that stood at his door waving a large white handkerchief until I was out of sight.

The next farm was also owned by a German, called Enrique, to distinguish him from Heinrich. He lived with a housekeeper, an Argentine woman with four children, the youngest ten months, and the conversation here was a bit more difficult, for it kept leaping between German and Spanish in a way that made my head spin. However, when the old argument was trotted out about the track to the Masters being too rough, I was able to counter, smartly, with Margret Geist, and finally Enrique said he would lend me a horse to go as far as the house of one of his shepherds, which was right on the boundary of the Masters' land. There I should surely find a couple of the Masters' horses waiting, he told me. If so, I should be all right. The going was so bad, however, that only the horses raised on the Masters' farm were ever able to tackle the track.

As soon as we had managed to explain all this to the housekeeper, she said that if I were going to Juanita's, she would come with me, as she had not seen her for five years, and we set off after lunch, leaving Enrique to cope with the four children by himself. We crossed a bog, then a swamp, and proceeded up a steep hill, reaching the top in such a gale of wind and rain that we were almost blown out of our saddles. The housekeeper, shouting at the top of her voice above the wind, told me that Juanita was a "*mujer muy rara*". Had the weather been better, I might have been able to get this statement elucidated, but as I was still puzzling it over, I caught sight of the house. A good-looking young man of about 23 or 24 came up to us, and was introduced as Juanita's husband, José. He welcomed us warmly, and as we approached the house, six children ran out, of whom the eldest was a girl of at least 14. José waved towards them and said proudly "My family." I supposed I had been unable to mask my astonishment because he added, rather hurriedly, "A family *communale*" and left it at that.

Inside the hut were five more children, three men, and Juanita herself, a cheerful, untidy woman of about 35, with very few teeth. She welcomed us in and took our wet things to dry by the fire. One of the men made *maté*, and this was actually the first time that I had it properly served. In a group of gauchos there is quite a ritual about it, one acting as a sort of high-priest. He drew out his silver-necked gourd and the silver *bombilla*, took a handful of *maté* from a cotton bag in his bedroll, and put it into the gourd. He then poured some cold water over it, felt about inside the *bombilla*, then took a good suck through it and spat vigorously on the floor. He then poured in some boiling water, took another suck, and filling it up again, handed it to the next person —always going from right to left. It was bitter and stimulating, and the heat took away the chill of the wet ride. I tried not to think about all the other mouths that the *bombilla* had been in before mine.

Juanita, in the meantime, was packing some of the smallest children into one of four bins serving as beds built into the walls of the hut, and shifting the sheepskin bedrolls of the three men, who, it turned out, had been with her for six days waiting for the launch. There was a large wooden table in the middle of the room; we sat round it while Juanita served us all with a generous, but very fluid meal, consisting of thin soup, followed by thick Scotch broth, and ending with large cups of strong, hot coffee, strained through an old sock. While we were very busy swallowing our dinner, a general discussion raged about my solitary journey to the Masters' farm. Jose declared that he had two of the Masters' horses, left by one of the gauchos who had been in to help with the shearing. The three men swore that I should never be able to do it, and must wait until the launch came. I said I could not wait any longer and was already a month late in starting, so I must go on in the morning without fail. *"No es posible esperemos aqui,"* said I, following this up by firmly banging my fist on the table.

After I thus asserted myself, we all turned in for the night. Juanita, José and three of the children in one of the bins, five children in another, and the housekeeper took the remaining three into her bin. I was hospitably given a bin to myself, and my half-hearted offers of taking a child, refused with courteous smiles.

CHAPTER FOUR
THE MASTERS

J OSÉ was up at daybreak saying that he would go out to catch the
Masters' two horses in the next paddock. He returned an hour
later, and after two cups of strong coffee, we set off in a gale of
wind and driving rain. The three men standing in a dejected
group round the doorway were calling "*Muy malo!*" after us, and I
must say that I felt they were quite right.

Huddled in my poncho, my face bowed over the saddle, I never
looked up into the wind and rain, as my horse followed José's
across the last pasture before the Masters' boundary, until we
halted to open the fence. We had come to a place where the rocky
hills ran down into the lake, and, wandering across them, our
track stretched out looking suitable for goats, for where it was not
rocky, the trail was thickly strewn with flints and stones.

On the steep rock-face we dismounted, allowing the horses to
scramble up after us in their way. Panting and blowing, their
hooves glancing off the flints, they came up like giant caterpillars.
Hours went by, the weather grew even colder, the track steeper,
the rain more penetrating, and the wind quite abominable. The
journey was misery, until, round a bend at the very bleakest spot,
we suddenly burst into a new world. About six miles away, the sun
was baking down on an expanse of glittering aquamarine. This,
then, was the icefield that stretches the length of the Cordillera,
extending about three hundred miles. Here and there, a
mountain peak thrust itself through. It was like a vision, and I
had a sensation of being the first human to see it. José, too, kept

nodding his head and saying *"Precioso."* We pushed steadily on, and, even when we lost the view, it would always return at the next bend. As we edged gingerly round a small cliff, José pointed to the summit and said that Margret Geist had spent a night there when she lost her way, and that she would have died of cold but for her dog.

The track began to descend, sharply, and José suddenly disappeared from view. There was no cry, so I cautiously urged my horse to follow, and he promptly sat down on his tail and shot off, with stiff forelegs, down a perpendicular slope to join the others, who were standing in the lake having a drink.

"This path in summer is under water," said José. That he should call it summer surprised me, for I had never associated summer with the kind of weather we were having. He advanced a little way, then turned round and came back, bursting into a torrent of Spanish. All I could understand was *"No es bueno"* and *"Imposible."* Indeed, it all looked impossible to me, so I just waited, woodenly, for him to do something. He walked his horse to a 20-foot rock, then went straight up it, leaping off at the top to stand peering over the edge. My horse, which had instinctively begun to follow, now had to stop, as there was no room for two of us at the top, and we seemed to be hanging almost vertically below him. At last he turned to me and said, "Follow me, but on foot!" and again disappeared from view. I was only too thankful to dismount, and as soon as we reached the summit, I slipped off and peered over. José was just below me, traversing another big boulder with a very nasty overhang, his trembling horse snorting his reluctance behind him. Grasping the reins in my hand, I hoped I should let go in time, if the horse fell into the lake, which appeared to be only too likely. We found ourselves again in the water, but this time on the causeway for which José had been looking. It was hewn from the stone, about three feet wide, and only above the water line in winter. Eventually, we arrived at a shepherd's shanty to find that he had, only the day before, fallen off the very boulder we had just climbed, into the lake, where his horse had given him a terrific black eye. We drank *maté* there and then started on again, the track improving all the time. As the view widened against the background of the glacier, I saw a thin plume of smoke coming from a little stone house — the very first I had seen in Patagonia — hugging the ground as though sheltering from the wind. There was a fast-running river beside it and a vegetable garden. I could see a second stone building and, as we came nearer, saw a white-haired man working on what turned out to be a sheep-dip. He looked as we came clattering up, showing a friendly, wind-burnt face and sparkling blue eyes.

"We were wondering when you would get here," he said, "but we never thought you would ride! Come right into the house. Mother will be so pleased to see you."

The little stone house was, in fact, quite large, but dwarfed by its magnificent setting. The walls were a metre thick, and it seemed almost like entering a medieval fort. Once inside, I was in England. Mrs. Masters, tall, slim and white-haired, must have been a great beauty when young.

"We heard there was a lady coming, and have been so looking forward to meeting you, but we never expected you today," she said.

"She rode in, Mother," said Mr. Masters.

"Another Margret Geist!" exclaimed Mrs. Masters. "She stayed with us for quite a while, you know."

"Oh, I am longing to hear about her," I said.

"Well, sit down, it's just tea-time, and you must make a good long stay, so there will be plenty of time to tell you all about her."

I sat down and looked about me. In spite of all that I had heard, I could still hardly believe what I saw. The Masters had been there for 40 years, and everything had been made by themselves. The strong stone house, with its thick wall, had been built while they were living in tents, during the winter's bitter cold. Seen through the frame of a three-foot-thick window-embrasure, the view from the windows acquired even more glamour. The chairs and tables were all made on the farm from home-grown timber. Even the sofa was stuffed with hair from the farm horses' tails. I picked up a broom from the corner.

"You did not make this, too?" I asked.

"Oh yes," she said. "Those are from the horses' tails too, and our son John makes all our shoes as well."

Tea was now ready, and she went to the door and rang a bell. Very soon, we heard the tramp of the homemade shoes, and two men came in. The son, though much taller than his parents, was easily recognisable, having the very same tranquil blue eyes; the other man, I think, was Mrs. Masters' brother.

It would be useless to deny that the Masters cast a spell on me from which I have never recovered. Their way of life seemed perfect to me. They had all the answers, and, excepting that so far they had no grandchildren, seemed completely happy. All round them, they could contemplate the work of their hands with unfailing satisfaction. They had not fought against nature so much as worked with her to wrest their livelihood from the wilderness. They had known very hard times — indeed, such a life must always be hard — but I felt convinced that they would unhesitatingly have done the same again, had they been offered the choice. Mr. Masters took me round the farm buildings. All, except one, was of stone. "In another ten years, it should all be finished," he said.

Up to now, the only people I had met had not been really entirely able to cope with the challenge that the climate and the isolation presented. Most of them were just getting by, and, in the case of many Europeans, were probably worse off than if they had never come out. Of beauty, they created nothing. For the managers of the big estates, it was different. They had the company behind them. To me, the only things that really count are those that we create for ourselves, and by ourselves, not for profit, nor even especially for others.

The Masters had had two children, but their daughter had died when she was 20. Their son was with them still. They had sent him to a boarding school in Buenos Aires, and Mrs. Masters seemed still surprised to be his mother. She would talk about him, telling me of all the things he was able to do, by the hour, frequently asking me not to tell him that she had done so. She showed me the beautiful riding-boots made from leather from their own horses, and the electric light system, run from a water wheel in the fast-flowing river by the house. In winter, it still functioned, sunk below the ice. We saw the irrigation system for the vegetable garden, carried overhead in hollow bamboo, that could be disconnected to deflect the flow into any particular plantation that needed watering. I learned also of his views on horse-breeding, and certainly he had succeeded in breeding animals that could cope with the almost impossible terrain in which the farm was situated.

One of the most remarkable things he had constructed was a camera, and he had taken some magnificent photos with it while on a trip with Padre Angostini, who was, oddly enough, the only priest I heard about while in Patagonia. He was an Italian and a keen mountaineer, so this region of Patagonia was the perfect parish for him, and there was hardly a peak of any size that he had not climbed. John Masters had shown him the mountains round their property and had climbed several peaks with him, taking most professional photos with his homemade camera.

The Masters' meals were superb; strawberries and cream, an unending choice of lovely fruit and vegetables from the garden, with home-bred beef and mutton. There was always stimulating talk, too, about the outside world, of Europe and the chances of war. Nor were they interested merely because war would inevitably bring them riches. Their thoughts ran more to problems of justice and necessity, in pleasant contrast to most of the other farmers, who were almost looking forward to war with its abundant profits.

Mr. and Mrs. Masters went to bed early, but sometimes John and I stayed up late, talking and arguing about everything under the sun, and it was almost impossible to believe that he had never left Argentina.

In the morning, Mrs. Masters was up at four o'clock, which was the reason that she could accomplish such an enormous amount, yet never seem busy. Cleaning the house, butter- and cheese-making, bottling fruits and vegetables, and a dozen other activities quietly filled her days, yet always left her time to tend the wonderful flowers she grew in a glassed-in verandah leading from the living-room. With her slight figure and gentle manner, it was frightening to think of the amount of work she actually accomplished.

Mr. Masters had once been a seaman, and had jumped overboard and swum ashore when his ship was off the coast of Patagonia 45 years before. He had spent a year with the local Indians, now entirely extinct, hunting rheas with bolas, and looking for gold. He had explored Lago Argentina, and as soon as he saw the northwestern end, decided that this was where he had to live. In those days, there was no question of buying land; it was not even claimed by any state. Taking with him the gold he had found, he worked a passage back to England and went to the farm in Devon where Mrs. Masters was waiting for him. Having described the place to her and the hardships, he asked if she thought she could live like that. "If you want me to, I will," she said.

Now, 40 years later, Spanish had infiltrated their conversation, and they described her home in Devon as "a pretty place, with a castle on top of a great *barranca*, the village in the *canyon* below." Mr. Masters told me all this as we were riding round the farm. The stone-built wool and shearing shed, sheep-dip and dam were lovely. There was no discordant note to divert my attention from the heavenly view, when I could see it, because from time to time it was completely blotted out by rain.

Mr. Masters listened with a smile to my ravings. "The Argentine government tried to get us out," he said. "They want to make this into a national park. They even offered me very good terms and a piece of land on the pampas with excellent grazing, and a road, from which I could have transported more sheep and soon paid off all my loans. I thought I ought to accept, but John wouldn't hear of it. Sometimes I think he likes the place even more than I do." His eyes swept over the mountains, the glacier, the stone buildings. "It will all probably endure for hundreds of years, but I am 64. I would like to see my grandchildren."

This was the secret wish of both of the old people, but it was so difficult for them to find the right girl. Mrs. Masters would invite the daughters of other farmers over to stay, because she said, quite untruly, that she needed the help. So far, all her efforts had been to no avail. John himself was too wrapped up in the place and his schemes for it, and he never went away. He rode with me one day to the glacier, where a kind of bamboo grew along its edge, and tiny bright-green parrots flew back and forth, and although he had known it all from babyhood, I could feel that the beauty of it always struck him anew — perhaps even more than it did me, seeing it for the first time.

I wished I could have stayed longer, and Mrs. Masters urged me to do so. "Margret Geist stayed for weeks," she said. "Poor thing! She was so thin when she came, but she put on two stone while she was with us."

Perhaps the prospect of gaining two stone crystallised my determination to tear myself away, for I had already become almost afraid of falling completely under the spell of this remote paradise. One morning I said goodbye, and set forth on a good Masters' horse for Lago Viedma to the north.

CHAPTER FIVE
THE PERFECT PICNIC MEAL

THIS time, the trail was not quite so hair-raising. All the riding about the Masters' farm on their horses had accustomed me to mountain-climbing on horseback. I found myself really in the foothills, always faced with a superb view; but the tracks were vile. The Masters had said that with luck I might well be able to pick up a *trupilla* at the next farm, owned by an Italian. He was delighted to have a woman visit him and made me a huge dish of delicious ravioli.

"Eat! Eat!" he cried, pressing helpings upon me again and again. "Where you are going there will be nothing but *asado*, there is no money there, only people running away from the police."

There was a small *trupilla* at his place. This is a group of horses, any number up to 25, driven by one man with the aid of a bell-mare. Sometimes the only horse he owns himself is the bell-mare, with a large bell hung round her neck. The other horses may be those he is taking away for grazing during the winter, when fewer horses are needed on the farms than in spring and summer — the time of the lambing, shearing and of the droving to the freezers. Occasionally they are young horses he is taking back to his own ranch to break in, or he may merely be horse-coping. Bartolomeo was the man in charge of this *trupilla*, and he promised to take me as far as a *boliche* on Lago Viedma. Ever since I had been in Patagonia I had heard about these *trupillas*, which were fast disappearing, as the country was becoming progressively opened up by roads.

44

"How long shall we take to get to the *boliche*?" I wanted to know. "Four days with a thin horse and two with a fat one," was the answer I got. Ours fortunately turned out to be fat ones. Much later I found out that Spanish-Americans also refer to "short" or "long" leagues, meaning those covered on a fat or a thin horse.

The horses were all corralled in a big paddock together with the bell-mare, a stout elderly soul with a lovely, deep-toned bell on a leather strap round her neck. We got up at sunrise, and Bartolomeo caught three of the horses and tied one up for me to saddle, one for himself, and one for our gear. By now I was just saying "*Del Norte*" when asked where I wanted to go. The only roads ran east to west and stopped slightly east of where I was. So long as I was going north it did not much matter to me where I went. The snow-covered Cordillera with the great glaciers lay to the west, impossible for horses. While I was saddling my horse, an operation that still cost me time and trouble, never having previously been obliged to do it myself, Bartolomeo had finished saddling his, and had collected a large bag of pebbles, the carcass of half a sheep, and some water in a bottle, all of which he tied to his saddle before I was ready.

These horses were going away for winter pasture. There were 12 altogether, and they were gay and frisky, snorting and kicking as they followed the bell-mare out of the paddock; she paid not the slightest attention to them as she loped along listening intently for Bartolomeo's cries telling her which way to turn.

For the first few hours Bartolomeo was kept going flat out. He had been picking up horses as he went north and had got three from my Italian host, but these all seemed reluctant to leave home. While the others cheerfully followed the lead of the bell-mare, the newcomers would keep trying to turn back. Bartolomeo would then bend low over his horse's neck and with a loose rein urge it to a gallop by murmuring into its ear. From time to time he took a pebble from his bag and, with perfect aim, threw it at the heads of the runaways so that they turned and rejoined the troop.

We stopped at midday and unsaddled our horses, turning them out to run with the rest, and collected some dry little shrubs to make a fire to roast our sheep's carcass and boil water for *maté*. We sat sucking the *maté* in turn while the *asado* was cooking. Bartolomeo was a careful cook, constantly turning the spit and tenderly sprinkling the meat from a bottle containing salted water with some chiles in it. He looked astounded at my ignorance when I asked what the bottle contained. *"Salza Inglesa,"* he said.

I could hardly refrain from snatching the meat from the fire, it smelt so inviting, and when the *Salza Inglesa* was added it was even better. At last he pronounced it done and handed me a huge hunk, which I held by the bone, gnawing off the meat with my teeth. He was more dainty, as he had a knife which he used to cut off strips of meat, but as he got nearer the bone, he gnawed away like me. It was really the perfect picnic meal and, indeed, I found I never tired of *asado* and *maté*, and certainly kept very fit on it. There was no washing-up and no litter because the bones, which were all we left, lay unnoticed among the many picked bones that strewed the ground.

That evening we camped out, and I was glad that the Italian had given me a sheepskin to put under my saddle; it made a splendid mattress nearly as good as foam-rubber. With the saddle behind my head as a windbreak, the sheepskin underneath me, and the poncho over my sleeping bag, I was superbly comfortable and slept like a log. However, I woke in the morning to find my poncho stuck to my face by my frozen breath, and not until we had revived the fire and I had taken my first good swig of *maté* did the circulation return to my nose and cheeks.

We breakfasted on cold meat and a cup each of strong black coffee before going off to catch the horses. Once Bartolomeo had caught the bell-mare, who was hobbled, the rest was easy. Bartolomeo had made it even simpler for me by leaving my horse with a long rope trailing from his headstall, so that I could catch the rope while still a good ten feet away from him.

As we rode, we passed herds of guanacos, who raised their heads and screamed at us. We saw several rheas running away, but one father with eight chicks too young to run far allowed us to pass quite close. The father rheas have a hard, anxious life as they not only help hatch the eggs, but sometimes also have to collect the eggs from the pampas, where the females have casually dropped them, to make up a worthwhile clutch. After they hatch out, the father is in sole charge.

That night we came to a section-shanty where an old Spaniard was living. He had been there for ten years without leaving once; only in the three months of summer did he have occasional visitors, so he was absolutely delighted to get two in one day. He sent his dog off at once to round up a sheep, then led me round his garden, spinning me a tremendous yarn of which I understood not a word. The dog soon returned herding a reluctant sheep which was instantly despatched, and Bartolomeo got busy making an *asado* while I was taken round the shanty. It was cosy and quite attractive, the walls being made of logs placed upright, side by side, and then chinked with sheeps-wool. A few rough planks were nailed to the logs as shelves, and the pride of our host's heart was his medicine chest. "*Estomaco muy malo*," he explained, placing his hand over it and hunching himself up with an expression of pain. In the medicine chest were three packets of bicarbonate of soda, each weighing two and a half kilos; the only other medicine seemed to be 12 bottles of Scot's Emulsion.

After a splendid *asado*, we rode on to the *boliche* at the eastern end of Lago Viedma, where the tracks from the coastal towns of Gallegos and Santa Cruz meet at their farthest point inland. In the *boliche* were 11 people, each of different nationality. One, a Danish woman, asked me in good English where I was going. I felt by now that I hardly knew myself but said, "I am trying to get up north, staying away from the roads and keeping as close to the mountains as possible. Bartolomeo who brought me here is going to Gallegos, so now I am hoping to make some new arrangements."

"Don't worry," she said, "I can help you. I have a very good friend who lives up at the northern end of this lake, and you must go and see her. Tomorrow you can come with me and I shall send you on to her." She told me her name was Thea.

As the *boliche* was run by women, we had the usual ghastly *puchero* for dinner, following by even more dreadful *tortas*. Everyone talked and shouted at the tops of their voices in various languages, but Spanish predominated. Cries of "Santa Cruz" and "Gallegos" reverberated round the room, and it looked at one moment as though knives were about to be drawn.

"What is it all about?" I whispered to Thea, who was taking it all very calmly. She smiled. "Oh, they are just discussing which town has the best *frigorifico*."

After the meal the sexes divided up; the men carried on their argument on one side of the room, while on the other the women moaned about the wind. Thea, who like me wore trousers, did not join in. The Spanish women were practically confined to their houses during the summer months, when a near-gale blows constantly between the hours of nine and five, making their skirts totally impractical. Indoors, the endless dreary howling of the wind becomes a strain on the nerves.

Thea and I were up very early. As we left, the women begged us to stay. *"Mucho viento! Mucho viento!"* they cried dismally, and the wind swooped murderously round the house making me quite nervous. Once we were out in it, however, it was so strong and steady that I could simply lean against it, resting my back. We jogged along a rough track to the river, passing an up-turned lorry in a ravine. It had been blown down there by the wind the previous week. We crossed the river on a raft pulled by four bullocks and rode the rest of the day through magnificent scenery, coming in the evening to a section house on Thea's husband's land. Here we spent the night, and next morning she sent me on to the Ramsdens with a peon as a guide.

Like the Masters' farm, the Ramsdens' was at the extreme limit of the grazing-land right in the foothills. It was bitterly cold, and bursts of driving rain that obliterated the view took all the pleasure away, for I knew we were crossing magnificent uplands. I was delighted when we came to a snug, green hollow below the hills and saw a low wooden house, a plume of smoke rising from the chimney. It stood in a small gay garden, surrounded by a fence, and faced us invitingly across the grass. As we cantered up, a child's voice called out, the door of the house opened, and a tall, slight woman with greying hair and sea-blue eyes came out. Behind her ran a pretty teenaged girl, her whole face alight with excitement at seeing strangers. I jumped off my horse and started explaining that Thea had sent me, but Mrs. Ramsden interrupted me: "We are so happy to see you. Beyond us are just the mountains, so we have few visitors. Welcome! Come in and do please stay as long as you can."

I followed her in through the brightly painted door into a huge kitchen, heart of the whole house. It was painted a clear, pale blue just like the colour of the sea off the coast of Denmark on a summer morning. There were white cupboards, and shelves with blue-and-white china. It was the nicest kitchen in Patagonia. We sat down at the table, and cakes and cups of coffee appeared like magic. We spoke in English. Both she and Kirsty, the daughter, spoke it almost perfectly.

"However did you learn to speak so well?" I asked her. "Have you been away to school?" Gerda Ramsden looked delighted.

"I invited the daughter of some English settlers to stay with us for the winter. She has only just left and, while she was here, we all spoke English. Next winter we have a German girl coming. Then we shall all speak German," she told me.

"What a wonderful way to learn languages," I exclaimed. "What do you do for the rest of the lessons?"

She looked a little distressed as she answered: "That is all I worry about. My husband and I, we love this life, but we chose it for ourselves. The children had no choice and we must be sure that they will be fit to go away if they want to one day. Kirsty is doing a correspondence course in Spanish and now she is starting to learn to use a typewriter."

Looking round the lovely kitchen through the window to the gay garden with a background of magnificent, snow-covered peaks, it seemed ridiculous to think that anyone should ever want to leave such beauty. But the lines on Gerda's face and her toil-worn hands betrayed the price she had paid. Again, I was struck by how much in these isolated places depends on the woman. Women like Gerda and Mrs. Masters worked minor miracles, and the results were enchanting, their houses and gardens blending in with the scenery and even adding charm to it. The Spanish women, both Chilean and Argentine, were usually hopeless, their one idea being to live as nearly as possible as though in a city. Any money they had would be spent on silk dresses rather than on their houses. In a way it was perhaps the simpler solution, as the only means of getting any shopping done was after the annual sheep drive to the freezing plant. From Gerda's house this meant a trek of 32 days to Gallegos, going at the sheep's pace of three leagues a day. The drovers could of course return much more quickly, but it was much easier for them to bring a few dress lengths than household goods. Another handicap from which Chilean and Argentines seemed to suffer was that they married so young, usually at 14 or 15, and that with a child every year they had lost much of their vitality and spirits by the time they reached 30. It needed a very great deal of hard work, time and thought, with unlimited co-operation and understanding from their husbands, to get results like the Ramsdens' and Masters'.

My thoughts were interrupted by the arrival of Hans Ramsden, a quiet, grey-haired man. The casual greeting they gave each other failed to disguise the deep affection between them. He was followed by Rudolf, their 18-year-old son. The kitchen for the next few minutes sounded like the tower of Babel. Hans greeted me in English, Gerda explained my arrival to him in Finnish, while Rudolf and Kirsty carried on a conversation in Spanish. We all fell silent, however, when Hans switched on the radio.

Each evening, the government radio broadcast messages, telegrams and news to all the settlers. It was a gigantic party-line throughout Argentine Patagonia. We could learn who had had a baby, whose son had passed his exam, and the price someone else had got for his sheep. At the end, Gerda said, "It is a wonderful thing for us and so convenient in time of illness. Like poor Mr. Bates; it was such a comfort for him when his wife died in hospital in Buenos Aires. He got the news the same day over the radio instead of having to wait a fortnight."

Next morning was cheese-making day. This was a speciality of Gerda's and she was quite famous for her cheeses. They netted the Ramsdens a fair amount of money too. Directly after breakfast, which was at dawn, the fire was stoked up and huge cauldrons prepared. Hans and Rudolf came rushing into the kitchen with pails full of still-steaming milk, which was poured straight into the cauldrons. Gerda tested the temperature by hand, able to feel unerringly the right moment to add the rennet and cut the curd. Then came the pressing of the curd. Gerda moved dexterously amongst the apparatus, occasionally giving me some simple chore to do. She also tried to explain it all, but it was difficult as she did it all by look and touch. She laid great store by the milk coming straight from cow to cauldron. Hans and Rudolf worked like demons, rushing the newly milked bucketfuls straight from byre to kitchen. As each cheese was finished, I carried it down to the cellar, already well stocked with others at various stages of the ripening process. The matured ones were round golden balls weighing about six pounds. Gerda made them with a thicker skin than normal as her customers needed a cheese easily carried tied to a saddle and above all impervious to weather.

By the time the last cheese was stacked in the cellar, we were all quite ready for a rest and as we sat round the kitchen table, I told them what I was hoping to do and asked them what the chances were of getting someone to go north with me. Hans looked doubtful. "It's getting late now, the weather is bad, and the only people who ever go that way are all wanted by the police."

Gerda was more optimistic: "What about that man Ramon Dias who came through in the spring? He told us he was coming back this way, bringing a *trupilla* to winter in the foothills." She turned to me: "If he comes, perhaps he would let you go with him."

It seemed all rather vague, but by now I was accustomed to uncertainty, and I had to admit that so far, something had always turned up, so I settled down to wait upon events and to enjoy such wonderful hospitality.

The next evening, a dapper little gaucho, a beret cocked sideways on his shining black hair, came riding up to the house. He bowed courteously and said Don Roberto was his name. "What is she?" he asked rather cuttingly, on being introduced to me. "A *turista*?" Rather embarrassed, I could only admit the impeachment, and Gerda came to the rescue by asking him where he was bound.

"I was on my way home when I met a shepherd who told me about Lago Solitaire. He said it was so beautiful that I too wanted to see it." He gave me a sly look: "If the *turista* would like to see it, I could take her too."

This seemed a chance too good to miss. "I'd love to go," I said to Hans and Gerda. "But what about the *trupilla*? Would it be safe to risk missing it?"

"Don't you worry," said Hans. "If Ramon comes while you are away, we shall keep him until you get back. I think I know where this lake is. With a really early start, you should be able to do it in a day."

We arranged to set off at daybreak, and Don Roberto retired for the night.

"How old do you think he is," whispered Gerda, as we watched him go.

"Oh, about 42," said I.

"No, he is 72, and last year he fell off his horse and broke his leg. He was quite ill for three months but now he is the same as ever."

It was still dark when we had our breakfast next morning, but the stars were beginning to fade as we rode off in search of Lago Solitaire. Don Roberto rode along very briskly. He told me he wanted to visit his old friend called Babby as well as to see the lake. Hans had given me a very good horse that easily mastered the difficult going, so I found myself able to keep up.

There was no track. We rode along, stopping every now and then while Don Roberto studied the landscape, muttering to himself. I supposed him to be repeating instructions given him by the shepherd, because usually after thus communing with himself, he would take a sharp turn to right or left. All this time we had been climbing steadily. Now suddenly we headed downhill and soon came to a river which we only just managed to ford, the rushing water coming up to the horses' bellies. On the other bank was the *monte*, or thick virgin forest. Here Don Roberto stopped and said, "It is very difficult, I think you cannot come."

I was so indignant that I said sharply, "If you can do it, so can I." As soon as the words were out of my mouth, I knew I had made an unfortunate mistake. He looked at me in silent disgust and, without a word, turned his horse and disappeared at a rapid lope into the forest. My horse, nothing loath, shot after him, and for the next few minutes I was in real trouble. Trees seemed to fly at me from all directions. At first I swung myself wildly from side to side, but after receiving some lethal blow from the branches, I tried crouching low along the horse's neck, my arm over my face to shield it. After what seemed several minutes of this, a smart blow on the back of my neck made me raise my head just in time to see an enormous branch coming for me. As it swept relentlessly down, I completely lost my nerve and flung both arms round it, the horse rushing on, leaving me dangling. With a convulsive heave, I managed to get my legs round the trunk also and, pulling myself into a sitting position, relaxed, my heart pounding. I was relieved to see that my horse had come to a standstill a few yards farther on, jammed by his saddle between two trees. Don Roberto, who had perhaps been paying more attention to his "*turista*" than I gave him credit for, came back and when he had got over laughing, disengaged my horse, and led him back under the bough on which I sat, and I dropped back into the saddle without a word. We then went on at a much quieter pace, at last breaking out of the forest and saw, across a stretch of soft greensward, a bright turquoise lake dotted with miniature icebergs, glittering and still in the sunlight.

In silence we both dismounted and walked the horses slowly across the grass. Mount Fitzroy towered above us, both its summit and the glacier reflected in the blue water. I almost had the feeling I was seeing a mirage; one false move and it would all vanish. Don Roberto must have had a similar feeling, for he slowly doffed his beret.

"It is beautiful." he whispered. "Rich people would pay a lot of money to see this."

We made a small fire and crouched beside it while we ate our sandwiches, our eyes ever drawn to the miraculous beauty of the lake. When a small chilly wind sprang up and a cloud covered the sun, Don Roberto got to his feet. "We must go," he said.

We caught our horses and went on through more forests until we came to a nightmare bridge. It consisted of four wire cables slung across the river, with boards laid on the two lowest. Nothing appeared to be fastened. Across this went Don Roberto mounted on his horse and in disdainful silence but with a look that spoke volumes, and I knew he was thinking of my unfortunate remark before entering the first *monte*. Leaving the reins loose and trying to interfere as little as possible with my horse, I followed him. The horses had obviously done this before; they put their heads right down between their knees, blowing apprehensively through their nostrils. Then, splaying their legs instinctively to lower their centre of gravity, they lurched uncertainly across. The whole bridge swung sideways in a sickening manner, affording me horrifying glimpses of the rushing torrent 20 feet below.

We rode on in silence until we reached Babby's shack, a small wooden box with a door and one window. Don Roberto dismounted, tied his horse up carefully and advanced to within three yards of the door, clapping his hands loudly three times. Nothing happened, so he went round to the back and repeated the performance. Again no result, so he looked about him and, picking up a few sticks, arranged them cabalistically on the ground in front of the house. Then, untying his horse, he began looking for a large stone to mount from. He was a tiny man and even on tiptoe could only just see across the saddle. "It is hard when you are small," he observed.

Thinking of Miles, I said rather proudly, "I have a friend who is two metres tall."

He gave me a shocked look: "How ugly! How ugly!" he muttered.

We had to negotiate the awful bridge again, but this time we dismounted and walked over, which was a lot less nerve-wracking.

It was late by the time we got back to the river we had forded that morning, and it had risen so high meanwhile that we were obliged to swim the horses. This was the first time I had done such a thing, and apart from the piercing cold, I must say I thoroughly enjoyed it. Don Roberto went first, telling me to copy him exactly. Leaning well forward in the saddle, he urged his horse down the bank and as soon as it started to swim, laid his cheek along its neck and stretched his legs along its rump. With his right hand he reached forward and gently splashed water in its downstream eye, thus keeping it heading sufficiently upstream to prevent it being carried away by the strong current. By the time we were across, we were both absolutely soaked, for although we were almost lying on the horses' backs, in the strong current little waves kept lapping over us. We trotted along, shivering and silent in our icy wet clothes, into the chilling wind until we came to a fence that needed opening. To my surprise, Don Roberto asked if I would mind opening it. "My poor leg suffers always from cold water," he explained. He looked pleased and very surprised when I managed fairly quickly to uncouple the wire and close it again behind us, and this evidently won me his entire forgiveness, for as we rode on, he started telling me about his accident, and by the time we eventually reached the Ramsdens in total darkness I had heard the saga of his entire life.

CHAPTER SIX
WITH RAMON DIAS

Two days later, Ramon Dias rode up with his *trupilla*. He was a small, dour Argentine, a horse-breaker by profession, but with the rapid growth of mechanisation, his job was becoming less and less important, and he was very bitter about it. He appeared to me to be the same age as Don Roberto but was actually only 34. It was one of the peculiar things about Patagonia: there were no young nor any old-looking people, they all appeared to be in early middle-age. Their life was so hard that they aged quickly, yet in order to keep alive at all, they had to keep fit enough to ride, camp and cut firewood, and so could not ever hope to cosset any rheumatism, arthritis or hardening arteries.

As we watched Ramon Dias unsaddle and turn out his *trupilla*, Hans said he might really be the man I was looking for. "All these people living in the foothills are running away from the police for some reason or another, but I know nothing against this man." On this slightly dubious note, he went off to talk to him and was back a little later with a smile. "He says he is so hard up that he will have to take you, although he does not like *gringas*."

Gerda laughed: "Really, you are lucky to get him. He is familiar with the whole country from here to Lago Cochrane, and as there is no road, there are also no *boliches*, so at least he cannot get drunk."

We went back into the house, and over supper discussed my plans. It was a wonderful chance for me, just what I had come to Patagonia hoping to find. Hans tried to temper my excitement by

55

saying that Ramon had insisted that I should agree to travel at his pace and to stop nowhere longer than he wanted to, as it was already late in the season for such a long journey. Ramon had, in fact, only stopped at the Ramsdens' farm to shave and have a bath. He did not intend to have another before next spring. He would be ready to start in the morning.

I enjoyed my last night in a bed and was too excited to be sorry over saying goodbye to Gerda and Hans next morning. Ramon and I were setting out on a trip of over 300 miles through virgin country, with ten horses and two dogs. We each had a pair of coloured woollen saddle bags for our clothes, and a large bag of *yerba maté*, a smaller one of coffee, some salt in a leather container, and half the carcass of a sheep.

The first day was very hectic, as the *trupilla* were wild and frisky, and as Ramon dashed after them, I would dash along too, as I was never quite sure at first whether he was just trying to round them up or urging us all on. By the time we stopped for lunch, I was getting the hang of it. We built a fire and unsaddled our horses and the pack horse, turning them loose with the others. Ramon did nothing for the comfort of his animal, but a mental picture of the other horses I had ridden, with grooms to rub them and cosset them after a ride, induced me to ruffle up the damp matted patch of hair under the saddle of my horse, and he really seemed to appreciate this little attention.

Ramon sharpened a piece of wood and stuck it in the ground leaning towards the fire with the meat impaled on it, and while it slowly roasted we sat drinking *maté*, giving the meat an occasional turn until it was nearly done, whereupon Ramon would dissolve some of the salt in boiling water and pour it over the meat. By the time it was roasted we were ravenous, and the two of us ate half a sheep a day whenever we could get it. Of course the dogs had some, but surprisingly little. After lunch we caught three fresh horses, saddled two for riding and put the pack on the third. Changing them at each stop, we rode them all in turn excepting for the bell-mare, who was treated as if she were sacred. This method saved them from the danger of sore backs or over-working them, since they had no food save what they could find on the trail. That night we camped out, having another *asado* for dinner.

Camping was very simple for we merely took the saddles off the horses and arranged them on the ground as beds. Ramon then started cooking the rest of the sheep while I gathered enough wood to keep the fire going, with a bit over to start it in the morning. About an hour after dismounting we were already asleep.

In the mornings everything depended on how easy it was to catch the horses. Breakfast itself was no problem; cold meat and a cup of terrifically strong black coffee. This morning the horses were co-operative, and half an hour after waking we were already jogging along an easy trail which led us, after about three-and-a-half-hours' ride, to what Ramon called a house. To me it looked more like a bird-watcher's hide. It was made of several skins stretched between the branches of a large tree and open to the north-east. It belonged to a friend of Ramon called Don Jorge.

Don Jorge had three dramatic-looking friends with him. All were wrapped in long, black capes with broad-brimmed black sombreros on their heads, and their remarkably small, narrow feet were incased in high-heeled boots with enormous rowelled silver spurs. Their manners matched their appearance. As each was introduced to me, he stood up and swept off his black hat with a gesture worthy of Sir Walter Raleigh, then bowed deeply over my dirty hand. Each one of them was a Don. To Ramon, the affluent, who earned their money by regular work such as station managers, were entitled to nothing better than the inferior "Señor". Ramon among his peers at last was a changed man, laughing and jolly. He even ventured a few jokes about taking me with him.

The four splendid Dons immediately began making an *asado*; one had the idea that I should prefer bread, and he produced a rhea's egg which he used to make a dough with flour that had been a long time in its sack. He finished by frying the lump in sheep's fat until it was quite indigestible, as I feared. Only the cook and I ate it, the other men saying that they had never in their lives eaten anything except meat and were not going to start now. I did not blame them at all; if I was going to spend my days on a restricted diet, roast meat and *maté* would certainly be my choice. It took all lunch-time for them to give Ramon messages to pass on to various friends he might meet on the way, and after the most stately farewells, we rode on for another four hours before camping. Ramon sent his dogs off to round up a sheep, which he killed and skinned. Making a little mound of stones, he placed the skin on it, putting more stones on top to prevent it being blown away.

"Why do you do that?" I asked.

"It is the custom. For food the traveller may kill a sheep but he must leave the skin for the owner." I was beginning to understand now how the people in the foothills managed to live. With a good dog and a knife they need never starve.

"Don Jorge and his friends, what do they do?" I asked.

"They work, for they must buy *maté*, but only for two months in the summer at one of the big stations. That is of course enough. Salt is the only other thing they must have, and that they collect at the edges of the bitter lakes."

It was a way of life too hard to me, I thought, but so very much better than many, and quite redeemed from brutishness by the ritual courtesy and the *maté* ceremony.

Next day it was piercingly cold, the wind quite demoniacal. It was the longest ride over the worst track I had ever known. Only the constant change of scenery, the sight of guanacos galloping all round us, their tails turned round like tea-pot handles, and the excitement of sliding the horses down perilous slopes kept fatigue at bay. When we got into the *monte*, all enjoyment ceased. As my horse slithered his way between the trees with no consideration whatever for his rider, my head, knees, elbows and feet each in turn received such tremendous cracks from passing trunks and branches that I was quite unable to avoid feeling a sneaking sympathy for peole who start forest fires. By the time we got out of the wood even Ramon was showing signs of strain. I was thankful when we stopped to camp on the first level ground we came to. An hour later we had eaten our *asado* and were snug in our beds. We slept well and awoke to find the ground covered with light frost. We wasted no time on breakfast, merely eating some cold meat as we jogged on our way. The going became easier as the day wore on, and the last stretch round the edge of Lago San Martin was quite lovely.

Indeed, towards evening we rode up a little knoll and looked suddenly down upon a scene that appeared to be straight out of the Grimm's Fairy Tales of my childhood. Against the traditional dark background of trees stood a long, brown log house, transported here by magic from the Austrian Tyrol. This sensation of reliving a fairy tale was even heightened when we got inside and I found myself sitting in a hand-carved chair near the comforting warmth of an enormous tiled stove, a big cup of perfect coffee with real cream in it in my hand, conversing in German with Hans Rennhofer, the Austrian owner.

We were both quite excited — he to have a visitor so recently arrived from Europe, and I to be warm and to recover briefly the joys of European culture and civilisation. We chatted of Austria, of the "Henerige" outside Vienna, of the theatres, of the streets lined with chestnut and lilac trees, of the charm and grace of the girls, and Hans said, "I just cannot understand these Spanish-American ones. All they seem to want is to have spectacles — not because they need them but because they think it is smart and makes them look clever. And as soon as they have got the spectacles, they want to have an operation on their appendix. Just imagine the type of girl who willingly gives up her virginity to acquire glasses and an abdominal scar!"

While we were laughing over this, Hans suddenly jumped to his feet saying, "With all this stimulating conversation I almost forgot the wireless news!"

He turned a knob, and we could hear the placid voice of the B.B.C. announcer describing Hitler's triumphal entry into Vienna, and the "Anschluss" as a foregone conclusion. Hans grew paler under his healthy tan as we listened in horror to an account of the troops marching along the Ringstrasse, wildly cheered by the populace, of tanks rolling over strewn flowers, bands blaring. Both of us secretly realised that this brought war another grinding step nearer. We parted for the night in crushed silence and, despite the warmth and comfort, I did not sleep as I had the last two nights on the freezing ground. It was almost with relief that I said goodbye to my charming host, as glad to flee civilisation today as I had been the day before to find it.

Right from the start the track was appalling; it led along the northern arm of the lake, with many short perpendicular slopes for the horses to shoot down. Ramon pressed on, and we halted only long enough to change horses and bolt down the sandwiches that Hans had given us. At dusk we came to a little clearing with a tiny shanty. Two men came running out when they heard the *trupilla*, an elderly man who was a Swiss prospector, and a quiet, gentle-looking Spaniard. No sooner had the Swiss discovered that I understood German than he poured out his hatred of Patagonia and the Patagonians. He was an unpleasant man, and as soon as we were inside the shanty I tried to get away from him by speaking

Spanish to the other man. But with my exhaustion and the strain of struggling with two foreign languages at the end of a long day, I must have become quite unintelligible.

As the Swiss was offering me the hospitality of the shanty, he asked whether I preferred eggs or meat, whether he should put my bed in the cupboard by myself or in the room with the men? The Spaniard stood gazing helplessly at me, murmuring at each suggestion, "Who knows, she may prefer *maté*," and when we were unrolling our bedding, took courage and loudly and firmly announced: "We will have a *maté* before we sleep," and promptly put the kettle on to boil. I jockeyed for a position next to Ramon as his teeth, in a land where tooth decay was rampant, were still fair to middling, and I preferred sucking the *bombilla* after the healthiest mouth in the group.

We made an early start next morning and found ourselves still struggling along the shore of the lake in the track of a forest fire. The wind whistling through the burnt stumps and scaly branches sounded like a storm howling through the rigging of a sailing ship. It gave the ride quite a nautical atmosphere, strengthened by frequent glimpses of the lake whipped into a frenzy of white crests. At about two o'clock it began to pour with rain. Bowed over my horse's neck and shivering with cold, I kept casting longing looks at Ramon's straight back for any signs of discomfort. At last to my delight he announced that he had a friend called Miranda who lived nearby and that we could go to him for shelter. The friend's house actually proved to be hardly more than a shelter. Miranda being away from home, only his large black cat welcomed us ardently, and we set about making ourselves comfortable, cutting a large hunk off the half-side of beef that hung outside to make a grand *asado*.

Next morning the weather was even worse, starting with a tremendous hail-storm that sent the *trupilla* flying off in all directions. It was two p.m. before we could round them all up again. There was no track and the going was terribly slow, with steep, slippery screes or perpendicular slopes, and the wind cut like iced daggers through our wet clothes. Ramon cursed and muttered, and it cheered me up to know that at least he too was suffering. But later, as it always turned out, we came up over a steep rise to see the Cordillera ranged in front, all covered in fresh snow, and this sudden flash of beauty stopped us in our tracks. Even when the cold drove us on and we ran into a shower of icy rain or reached a cliff so sheer that we had to scramble down coaxing the horses, that beauty still stayed with us, making it all easy. Later we rode through the *monte*, but here the trees were taller, and I could sit up straight in the saddle and look about me.

In soothing silence, my eyes freed for the first time that day from wind-engendered tears, I rode along the faint track behind Ramon. Suddenly a slight movement caught my eye. There between two trees stood a *muerale*, a little mountain deer, a species now almost extinct. I saw two small antlers, a brindled, bristly coat, and two large eyes that stared fearlessly at me. Entranced, I dismounted, walking slowly towards him, and was almost within touching distance when Ramon came hurtling back in a high rage, thinking that I had lost my way. In a flash the muerale was gone, but as soon as I explained what I had been doing, Ramon's rage immediately evaporated. He had no patience whatever with injuries or exhaustion but was genuinely interested in wildlife and scenery. "How lucky you have been to see one. Men I know who have lived here for years have never had your luck." He shook his head sadly as he spoke, and I could see that he felt it to be a grave injustice.

We had to cross briefly into Chile, and Ramon was always looking for something to disparage while in Chilean territory: when we came upon a 14-year-old girl with a three-month-old baby living by herself in a shack of roughly built tree trunks placed upright in a trench and roofed with skins, he pronounced loud and clear, while the poor child clutched her baby, staring at us with terrified eyes: "Chilean women are not civilised, they are never taught manners like our Argentine ones."

The poor girl on hearing this managed a whispered invitation to take *maté*, and Ramon immediately sat down, waiting like a lord while she prepared it. Her husband, she told me, had gone off three days before and she did not know when he would return. I could not help hoping it would be before she finished the quarter of beef that he had left hanging in a tree for her. Our *maté* finished, we said goodbye. I should have felt guilty at leaving her alone but for the fact that she was so patently anxious for us to go. We resumed our rain-sodden ride through bog and forest. Ramon said that we must press on since we had already lost so much time, yet when towards evening we sighted a shanty, Ramon's rigid code of etiquette would not let him pass it without calling.

61

Three men came out to greet us with ceremonious bows and formal speeches, their flashing smiles and shining eyes showed how delighted they were to have visitors. No sooner had Ramon told them that we could not stay long, as he wished to reach Loco's house before dark, than they firmly said, "Loco has left as there is no grazing, so there will be no food either. You will have to stay with us." On closer inspection, the shanty turned out to be the best we had seen. It had two rooms, a front door with a hatch for the cat to get in and out, and quite a lot of hand-made furniture, including a narrow bed that looked exactly like a coffin.

The three men were completely dissimilar. One might have been out of an El Greco canvas, his pale, gaunt face shadowed by a large sombrero. The second man was a short, stocky, one-legged Chilean, and the third man was so startlingly black that it took me a moment or two to notice that he was also almost a dwarf, with a huge head crowned by a battered sombrero below which his teeth flashed dazzlingly white when he smiled. As we squatted round the fire for *maté*, each man was working away on a piece of hide, each at a different stage of curing. One was kneading a piece, working it gently back and forth between his hands and stretching it across his knees to soften it; the Chilean was scraping the last vestiges of fat off another piece, and the black dwarf was busy rubbing the brains of a dead animal into a third piece. Every now and then one would stop to caress and talk to a sleek ginger cat. There was such a pleasant atmosphere of unhurried efficiency that fatigue dropped off me like a coat.

A curious call from outside brought us all to our feet. The Chilean opened the door and through it I glimpsed, riding out of the dusk, another El Greco figure leading a most pitiful animal, a horse with a hideous gaping wound in its belly out of which trailed some of its intestines. It could barely totter, and the man led it to a tree on which half a side of beef already hung, then drawing his knife he swiftly slit its throat, and we all stood silent, watching till it died. The men then burst into furious activity, cutting the skin in a circle round the haunches and drawing it down the leg, like pulling off a stocking, cutting it free at the top of the hoof. These would make a pair of waterproof, knee-high riding boots. The carcass then was cut up and the hide scraped and pegged out. One of the El Grecos cut a hunk off the wild beef carcass and we went back into the hut to make an *asado*. While the one-legged Chilean cooked, the others sat round in a sinister-looking circle, sharpening their knives and exchanging news with Ramon of mutual acquaintances. Most of these seemed either to have met sudden grisly deaths from knife fights when drunk, or had suffered from gangrene setting in after accidents like broken bones, or else they had been impaled on broken branches like the unfortunate horse.

When I murmured something about doctors, they all looked at me in utter astonishment. The dwarf gave his flashing smile and, pointing to the Chilean, said, "He is a doctor, he cut off his own leg."

They were all plainly amused at my amazement, and the Chilean, although pleased over my admiration, obviously considered me to be over-emphasizing his remarkable courage. "But why was that bravery?" he said. "The pain from the gangrene was so bad I could only cut the leg off or kill myself. I was only 20 and I did not want to die." He gave his wooden leg an affectionate pat: "Now it can never hurt me anymore," and he immediately turned his attention to the *asado*, dissolving some salt in boiling water and trickling it gently over the meat. At the sound of drops falling on the fire the rest stood up, carefully removing their hats, mealtimes being the only time, except in bed, when gauchos are bareheaded.

After dinner there was no washing-up since no utensils had been used, each of us employing his own knife to eat with. There was a short discussion as to where I should sleep, and the coffin-bed was carried into the second room for my use. When I lay down, the 18-inch-high sides cut off all visibility, but in spite of not being able to bend nor to turn round at all without first sitting up, I was soon asleep. Later I was awakened suddenly by the most extraordinary noise penetrating the wall of my coffin. In inky blackness I felt for my torch and, sitting up, switched it on. There on a sheepskin on the floor, his cheek pressed against my bedside, his open mouth making a groaning noise, lay the black dwarf. The light woke him and he gave me one of his toothy smiles. "I guard you, you can sleep in peace," he said, and so we finished the night, our cheeks only separated by the thick coffin wall.

We left early next morning after a good meat breakfast and with a parting present of a hunk of horse-meat. We rode through wonderful scenery. Blue glacier lakes like turquoise enamel, and blood-red rocks. "How beautiful it is," I said to Ramon.

"Of course," he replied. "We are now back in Argentina."

We were gradually emerging from the *monte* but had not yet reached the plain. All round us the red-breasted wild geese were so tame that I could get to within five feet of them. When night came we camped in pouring rain under the largest tree we could find, the geese roosting in the branches above us, and woke sodden and very hungry. Our hunk of meat had shrunk so alarmingly that we only ate one small slice with our *maté*. Now the sun came out to cheer us, and we jogged along as briskly as our horses could manage for they, poor things, had been unable to find any grazing during the night. We came to some depressing bogs and as we struggled through them, I was unpleasantly reminded of *Pilgrim's Progress*. Sheer purple and dark-red mountain slopes dipped into glittering expanses of glacier all around us. At the foot of an enormous black scree lay a bright-green pool. Duck and geese circled overhead as our exhausted horses slipped and staggered through the bog.

After an interminable four hours, Ramon's horse got badly bogged for the second time and we gave up and camped out in cold, wet misery, nibbling on lumps of cold meat, it being too wet to light a fire. I reflected how often on the journey out from London I had been longing for just this sort of thing, but now that I had got it, it was the discomfort after all that dominated everything.

Daybreak was perfect. The sun rose on a world powdered with glittering snow, but all this light and brightness seemed slightly dimmed by a piercingly cold wind which did, however, help to dry our clothes. Today we were climbing all the time and, with each added foot of altitude, the wind grew colder and colder until towards mid-morning it started snowing.

Finally we reached the pass and changed direction, plunging steeply down with the wind behind us. I relaxed and leant back against its steady thrust as though I were in an arm-chair and closed my eyes. A sudden gust and crash and I was lying on the rocks below, my horse standing six feet away pitifully regarding me through a halo of sheepskin and saddle, the stirrups hanging like grotesque earrings down each side of his head. I had been blown clean over his ears, after which Ramon, looking very disgusted, suggested walking the horses, and I was thankful. So we struggled down, leaning back against the wind until we came into more *monte* and suddenly the wind was gone. There was silence and a feeling of warmth, and all sorts of comforting familiar sounds began to make themselves heard again. Beyond the *monte* we came to a valley so thickly strewn with bones that the horses' hooves rattled through them in the most macabre manner.

By evening we reached a police outpost. Here to my horror were women, and as my thoughts ran almost exclusively on food, I knew this meant that unappetising *puchero*, the dreary dish of meat boiled to a tasteless rag. But the policemen were wonderfully sensible. Realising that their women were hopeless cooks, they drove them firmly into the house while they built a grand fire and made an *asado* outside. The two women surprisingly had only one child each, a rather grubby girl of about eight, and a jolly baby of five months that sat on his mother's lap during the meal and accepted with cries of delight well-masticated morsels of mutton offered straight from her own mouth. Occasionally someone else, happening on a particularly succulent piece, would give it a rapid chew, offering the resultant mess to the baby, who was invariably charmed. After the meal we started preparations for bed, and to my consternation the mother of the eight-year-old vacated her place in one of the two beds and went in with the baby and his mother, leaving me her daughter, some very dubious sheets, and a beautifully clean cat. Hearing the rain pouring down all night made me enjoy it much more than I had expected.

Day broke but the rain went on and on. By this time I was accustomed to these delays and, fully realising the value of constant snacks, eagerly accepted any food offered to me. By eleven the rain had died down to a light drizzle and we left. There was not a breath of wind; the horses stepped in uncanny silence across a land of lava and shells. Guanacos galloped all round us, one old bull having great trouble with his eight wives, who played a kind of Grandmother's Steps with us, running up behind our horses until we turned our heads and they saw our faces. Then they would stop dead and pretend to be grazing. After about a mile of this, the old bull got fed up. He galloped across in front of his harem, turned with a snort to face them, throwing himself on his knees and shaking his head. This was apparently a very serious threat because they all obediently turned and galloped away.

We rode along in windless peace, the wonders all around us sinking gently into my consciousness. Movement seems to help me to appreciate beauty, and the horse's jog-trot, now that I had mastered it, was pleasant enough. We came upon another turquoise-blue lake almost halved by a projecting peninsula. On the other side the land looked like a highly coloured picture of intestines out of a medical text-book. At our feet ran a river on a bed of pink, green and mauve stones. At 7:30 in the evening we stopped to camp, but our supper was only *maté*, as the police had not given us any meat. I crawled into my sleeping-bag and began brushing my hair before going to sleep when a horseman came jogging up with half a sheep carcass across his saddle.

"I saw you from over there," he said, his arm sweeping a gesture toward the plain, "and knew that coming from the mountains you would be hungry," and he bowed to me: "Francisco Reyes at your service!" He carved a large chunk of meat off the carcass and with another low bow, laid it at my feet. I sprang out of my bag babbling my thanks, while Ramon blew at the embers of the fire. We pressed *maté* on him and invited him to eat with us, and there we sat until midnight by which time we had eaten the original gift of meat and most of the rest that he had been carrying. At last even Ramon felt gorged and when Francisco offered us his last morsel, we said we had had enough. He got to his feet and bowed. "*Buenos noches, Señorita,*" he said. Although I had never heard a Spaniard actually say it but had only read it in books, I felt moved to say with heartfelt gratitude: "*Vaya con Dios.*" He gave me a startled glance and rode hurriedly off into the night.

I fell asleep like a log but the first light of dawn brought Ramon to his feet and keen to start. A light rain was falling and it took us nearly two hours to coax up a fire for *maté* and to catch the unfortunate horses that had been wandering miles in search of food. At last, glum and soaking, we plodded off towards the intestinal-looking landscape. The rain got lighter and the sun peered morosely through the clouds. The way was rocky and depressing.

In spite of last night's feast we were again famished with hunger, and I was trying not to think about food when we rounded a huge boulder and came upon a man skinning a sheep. He offered us some ribs and our spirits revived. The news that the path had been swept from the hillside into the torrent below did not upset us, although the horses were sweating with terror as they traversed the now practically vertical slope of mud-covered rocks. Later we trotted briskly down to a little valley where we built a fire against a large pink boulder. Sitting on two mauve rocks we sucked our *maté* while the gorgeous smell of roasting meat filled our nostrils, and I reflected upon how rapidly one's life can become entirely governed by only three needs — food, warmth and sleep — to the total exclusion of all else.

Perhaps because this was on our last day, for we were now on the borders of a large *estancia*, Ramon became much more human. He pointed out an armadillo that happened to be passing and gave me his candid opinion about anything and anybody not Argentine. In common with most of his countrymen, he was quite fanatical on the subject of Argentinian superiority.

"But the Chileans have been so kind to us. They are a good people," I protested.

"As good as can be expected from such a poor country," was his austere reply, and he shot to his feet saying that we must leave at once, forgetting perhaps that we had already crossed the border.

We arrived late that night at the *estancia* and to Ramon's disgust, although it was in Argentina, it was owned by a Canadian. He was elderly, tired and friendly, his wife round and welcoming. She took me straight into the kitchen, so clean, colourful and comfortable that it seemed to swing me into another world. She gave me a steaming cup of coffee, a slice of homemade chocolate cake and then took me to a room with a bed with clean sheets and coloured blankets, understandingly remarking, "You look far too tired to wash." Already dropping with fatigue, I was asleep in a few minutes, but in the morning Ramon was anxious to be gone. The civilised atmosphere I was enjoying so much quite disgusted his Spartan temperament. When I paid him for bringing me safely all that way, he never even looked at the money; he just put it straight into his pocket, giving me a haughty stare when I suggested that he count it to make sure if he were satisfied.

After this sordid business transaction was over, he thawed for a few minutes and shook hands with me, saying when I thanked him for showing me such beautiful country, "If you like it so much, you should marry and stay here." This I accepted as a great compliment. Then without a backward glance, he jumped on his horse, cracked his whip in the direction of the other two and jogged off back towards the border lands. Actually, we had made excellent time considering the conditions, the climate, and the absence of trails — more than 300 miles in 15 days.

CHAPTER SEVEN
ACROSS THE LAKE

THE Macleans, on whose *estancia* I was staying, were wonderful to me. But after a couple of days spent in washing myself, my clothes and my hair, and cleaning my saddle, not to mention positively stuffing myself with Mrs. Maclean's wonderful food, the old urge to push on assailed me.

It was already mid-March, and winter was overtaking me from the south. I got out my map of Patagonia to find out exactly where I was, and there, on the western side of Lago Buenos Aires, I saw a large, white blank on the map. Some of the regions I had come through with Ramon were also white on the map, but the trouble was that I could never be quite sure where we were until we got to a lake that had a name, so felt that I could still hardly claim to have been in totally unsurveyed territory. Here, however, it was a case of pushing on anywhere west of Lago Buenos Aires. If I could only do a trip on that side, I should be able to brag with confidence about travelling across a blank on the map.

When I told the Macleans about my great plan, they laughed. "Well, the map-makers may think it's a blank, but you would find it full of law-dodgers," said Mr. Maclean. "However, I can see that they might consider it an adventure in England." Dashed but not disheartened by this remark, I said I was keen to try it anyway.

"Well, the best thing you can do is to go to Lucas Bridges. His *estancia* borders the whole frontier and the southern shore of Lago Buenos Aires. He would love to help you carry out this crackbrained idea. We can lend you a horse to go to his place."

Lucas Bridges, I knew, was a name to conjure with in Patagonia. In Buenos Aires I had first heard of him, and again in Santiago, Chile, and, more frequently, in Patagonia. I had not realised that I was so near to his *estancia*, nor that he was still living on it. I could form no real picture of him from all I had heard, yet no man, I felt, could really be quite so wonderful as the reputation which he had.

Son of a missionary who had been sent to work among the Indians in Tierra Del Fuego and who had resigned after an argument with his superiors, Mr. Bridges felt that just teaching Christianity was not enough. The Indians should first be taught how to cope with the new civilisation brought to them by the invasion of European sheep-farmers. As Mr. Bridges' independent views lost him his income as well as his job, he took up some land and, with the aid of his family and some of the Indians, started sheep-farming.

When he was just 14, Lucas had been sent off by his father to an outlying part of the *estancia* to spend the six months of winter looking after several thousand sheep. He took with him only a bag of rice and a gun. During those six months he had relied entirely on himself, hunting and cooking his own food and building his own shelter against the Antarctic winter. This Spartan adolescence had certainly borne fruit, for he was now one of the wealthiest *estancia*-owners in Argentina.

I was glad to have a legitimate excuse for going to see him, so I simply jumped at the opportunity, and with a good horse and a plan of the track, I started off. Now that I was back among good farmers, it was much easier for me to find my way alone. There was quite a fair rough road, and all the fields were fenced, with a particular type of stile, near the gates, for horsemen to negotiate without dismounting. As mounting was still my greatest weakness, and as Argentine horses are usually expected by the gauchos to give a few bucks on being mounted, the prospect of the stiles gave me great confidence. I felt rather pleased with myself as I said goodbye to the Macleans, although they obviously considered it to be nothing out of the way.

I soon got out of the brightly coloured land and was then on the Bridges' property. The fences stretched for miles, ending only where they reached cliffs too steep for sheep. Every now and then I could see literally thousands of sheep being moved. Had they not been dirty white, it would have looked as though the earth itself were moving. Around the edges of these vast flocks, the tiny little sheep-dogs could be heard, but only occasionally seen, sometimes flying along with a front paw tucked up in their collar to stop them using a cut foot. Only towards evening did I see the house, quite small and unpretentious, but well-built and absolutely windproof. As I rode up towards it, the door opened and a tall, grey-headed man, with enormously long arms, came down the steps. He had a rugged face, but it was a peculiarly quiet voice that said: "You must be Miss Boxer. I was hoping that you would call."

He proved to be a comfortable person, and I immediately felt that I had known him for years, finding him even better than the most wonderful stories about him. It was two o'clock in the morning before we stopped talking, and by that time we had got to the stage of putting a clock on the table between us so that each had an alternate half-hour for airing our views.

After my ride with Ramon, and seeing how much better the bachelors lived in the bush than the married men, I was very worked up about the women. They should be educated, I announced, then they would be able to use to advantage the money their husbands earned on the big *estancias* in the summer. There was no valid reason why the South American woman should not have as comfortable a home as the European settler, if she could only be taught how to go about it. Lucas, his face creased with laughter, said: "Tomorrow I am having a lunch for the wives of some of my overseers. You will have to give them a talk."

"Of course," I promptly answered. But next morning I found that he was really expecting me to do so, and in Spanish. My heart sank, but I felt that somehow he was going to judge me by it, whether in fact I was one of those people who only talk and never do. So I spent an absolutely agonizing morning with my dictionary, trying to find suitable Spanish words for a talk on child-marriage, birth-control and education. All subjects very far removed from my previous Spanish conversations.

The lunch was delightful; that marvellous Spanish courtesy helped me to falter through my speech, and as my dreadful Spanish stumbled out of my mouth, no one even smiled. Perhaps they did not understand a word. Lucas was purple with suppressed laughter, but I was exhausted when I sat down to waves of applause. One woman had understood a little, and we had a more easy talk afterwards, but I realised that it would be a Labour of Hercules to get the customs changed unless the men themselves took an active part in the transformation.

The men were always keen enough to strike for better conditions on the big *estancias*, demanding showers, good bunk-houses and proper cooking arrangements. Then, having worked all summer in comparative luxury, they seemed perfectly satisfied to return to a home consisting of a few tree-stumps stuck vertically into a trench, the gaps between roughly chinked with sheep-wool, and a roof of branches, scraps of hide or slivers of wood, without a chimney, water or any lavatory; without a stove, but with plenty of cold, wind and snow.

In order to keep alive, a fire must always be kept burning day and night. To bring anything between six and 17 children into a world dominated by such conditions is enough to crush the spirit of any woman. Married usually at about 13 or 14, a young girl will simply move from the shack of her parents to the possibly even more primitive one of her husband. She will almost certainly have her first baby in the first year and, therefore, get no chance to see any other way of life — magazines and books being rarer than miracles.

That evening I broached the subject of my proposed ride round the west side of Lago Buenos Aires. Lucas' reaction was the same as the Macleans'. "It may be a blank on the map, but it has quite a few inhabitants, and the country, I hear, is more suited to boats than to horses. But it might be an interesting thing to do." He paused, then went on: "I shall be going to one of my out-stations tomorrow; there are several men from Chiloe who will be coming in to be paid off. If one of them agreed to go with you, you might make it. I have a launch that usually takes them to the northern part of the lake, and from there they ride to Puerto Aysen. You come out with me tomorrow and stay at the station until the men come in, which will be any day now. Then you must arrange it all yourself. It will not be an easy trip, and I certainly do not want them to feel that I am making them go. You can rely on me for horses, though."

I was in a hopeful mood as we set out next day at dawn to ride over to the out-station. Lucas sat slackly in the saddle, his big body swaying to the movement of his horse, while he told me how tired he had got in World War One, in which he had served as a gunner, when he had been made to rise to the trot.

Some years after meeting Lucas Bridges, I met a man in Calcutta and somehow the subject of my South American journey came up. He said, "I remember meeting an amazing man from Patagonia called Bridges while I was with the Gunners in World War One. I shall never forget how I saw him for the first time when one of the limbers had got stuck in a shell-hole. The horses were badly bogged too and could not pull it out. There were three of us struggling to get the wheel free when this enormous man rode up to ask what was wrong. He looked surprised that we could not move the limber and, getting off his horse, took off his tunic and, gripping the wheel with both hands, lifted it out of the hole as though it weighed a couple of pounds."

As we jogged along talking, his eyes were taking in every detail of the land, the sheep and the condition of the fences. He absolutely delighted me by suddenly dismounting to pick up a nail he had noticed lying on the ground. He showed it to me with pride, saying, "It is a good one, it's never been used. Must have dropped off the pack-pony on the way to the shepherd's hut."

We rode on all day, but with no stop for *asado* or *maté*, until we reached the section house where an Englishman, Mr. Lancaster, was in charge. It was quite a little settlement, complete with sawmill. Mr. Lancaster lived in his own house with a housekeeper, Mrs. Figueras, and her husband, who worked at the mill. Lucas only stopped long enough to despatch his business and have a *maté*, a sandwich, and change horses, then he was off again. By the time he got back to his house, he would have done about 18 hours riding. The atmosphere seemed a little strained until he left. Being such an exceptional person himself and having been brought up in such a hard school, he did not fully realise how difficult it was for others to attain his perfectionist standards, and they well knew that nothing would escape his notice, no matter how casual he seemed.

Mr. Lancaster was quite young, only about three years out from England, and still seemed a bit bewildered by Patagonia. The sudden arrival of an Englishwoman appeared to cause him acute embarrassment until the joy of not having to speak in Spanish finally put him at ease. Mrs. Figueras, jolly and shapeless, was terribly distressed about dinner and insisted that we must have a chicken. "Have they roosted yet?" asked Mr. Lancaster.

"Si, si, Señor!"

He reached down a couple of 22 rifles, giving one to Mrs. Figueras, and they went off together to a clump of trees where the hens were perched. After a couple of shots they came back with a plump hen, shot by Mr. Lancaster; Mrs. Figueras, having only wounded one very slightly in the leg, they decided to leave it for another day.

Mr. Lancaster thawed a little during the meal and plucked up courage to give his honest opinion of my plan to travel up the western shore of the lake. "You are crazy to think of it, and I can't understand Mr. Bridges letting you try it. It's all either virgin forest or bog, and not long ago there was a very bad forest fire. You can still see it smoking in places. However," he added with a definite look of satisfaction, "I don't think you will get any of the Chileans to go with you. They always take the launch to the north arm of the lake and ride up the Argentine side of the border till they reach the Puerto Aysen road."

"You don't think that one of them would come with me instead of going on the boat?" I asked.

He looked at me pityingly. "Of course, some of them might *say* they would, but how long they would stick by you, I should not like to say."

In the morning the first gauchos began coming in to fetch their pay before leaving, but none of them would even consider going with me. They had been working all summer so they had no urgent need of money and were in a hurry to get back to their families. By the time the first five had come and gone again, I was feeling rather depressed, and the "I-told-you-so" look in Mr. Lancaster's eye did not help.

Next day a few more men came in, but still I could get no one interested in coming with me. I had now been three days at the sawmill and was getting thoroughly discouraged. The weather, which was perfect — indeed the best since I had been in Patagonia — only made me think how far I might have got, had I only been able to start. I did not like to venture too far afield for fear of missing the chance of meeting a man who would come with me, and in the house the conversation ran continuously on the chances of war in Europe. I had found this a favourite topic with the majority of ranchers, and most of them, secretly if not openly, welcomed it, since it would mean a boom in the price of wool.

Their hopes had already been raised by recent heavy purchasing by the Japanese. Being in love with a soldier and coming from a military family brought up on rather old-fashioned ideas of giving one's life in defence of one's country, this purely commercial aspect of war upset me. It was, therefore, in the lowest spirits that I responded to Mrs. Figueras' call to tea.

As I walked towards the house, I noticed a gorgeous figure ride up. He was wearing a broad-brimmed black hat. His smooth brown face was embellished by a pair of magnificent black moustachios. A bright woollen belt was round his waist and huge silver spurs fixed to his slender boots. Over his shoulder hung a black poncho. He was talking to an obvious Englishman, looking very matter-of-fact and unglamorous in a baggy old tweed coat and trousers. They were introduced as Captain Williams, skipper of the lake launch, and Don Hernandez from Chiloe.

As we sat down to tea I tackled Hernandez about coming with me, and, to my joy, he did not refuse outright, and Mr. Williams suggested: "I've got the launch at the Rio Baker. You can ride over there and I can take you across the river and drop you on the western coast. You can see what it is like, and I'll be coming back in a couple of days, so if you get into any difficulty, just make a smoke signal and I could pick you up."

This offer had a wonderful effect on Hernandez, and it was not difficult to persuade him to give it a try. I then gave him some money to seal the bargain.

In the early morning, the three of us started off for the Rio Baker. I had a good sturdy horse, and so had Hernandez; we did not have a pack horse, as we thought that, with the poor grazing, the fewer horses the better. Mr. Williams said that he would get the gear I could not take with me across the lake and deliver it to the *estancia* of the Fugellies. I would have to make my way to them — if and when I should succeed in getting round the lake. Hernandez seemed quite happy, but Mr. Lancaster prophesied doom. "I do hope you'll be all right, but you never know how these chaps will turn out. Good luck to you! Believe me, you'll need it!"

Nothing could damp my enthusiasm, however, and I refused to be put off by Mr. Williams, who was now rather dismal, muttering about: "Nothing but bogs and runaway convicts, or else forest fires." Hernandez, taking a quick look at his face, also started murmuring: *"Quien sabe? Como no?"* We all brightened up when we got to the Rio Baker, for there was the launch called *Andes*, and a *boliche* run by a Syrian, who, judging by his condition at that hour of the morning, must have been his own best customer. We all had a drink and Hernandez bought a tin of evaporated milk, which he presented to me with a low bow and a flourish.

The *Andes* was a small, old, but serviceable-looking boat with a tall funnel that vomited clouds of smoke. The horses were hoisted on board with slings, and in a remarkably short time we were under way. The scenery was superb. Great snow-covered mountains stretched away on the left with rich green forest spread below them. Closer to the shore we could see many blackened stumps, victims of the forest fire. As the launch chugged along close in shore looking for a place to land us, I could see that a lot of ground was smothered in pale fine ash left by the fire. It was a sinister-looking coast, and rather to my alarm, Mr. Williams said cheerfully, "Looks O.K. to me! Shall we drop you here?"

I turned to Hernandez. He heaved a deep sigh. *"Como no?"* he said.

At once the wretched horses were picked up in their slings and lowered overboard into the icy water, where they struck out for the shore; the dinghy that we had been towing astern was hauled alongside, Hernandez and I got in, and Mr. Williams waved cheerfully. "I'll be back this way the day after tomorrow. If you are in difficulties, make three smokes."

We joined the horses on the stony, inhospitable shore and, with friendly toots, the *Andes* steamed away. I felt rather like an abandoned mutineer, and Hernandez did not look as if he were feeling much better, as in silence we set about loading the horses. There seemed no point in trying to ride them as we were in a perfect maze of trees and deadfalls. So we blundered about the edge of the lake for two hours and then decided to camp as it was getting dark. The best thing about this dismal place was the amount of easy-to-get firewood, and we had a good blaze going in no time. Sitting with strong cups of coffee in the bright firelight, we soon began to feel more cheerful about the next day.

We were up bright and early and spent the whole morning looking for a track. Although this was just the sort of thing I ought to have expected in a blank on the map, I was unreasonably infuriated. Eventually Hernandez announced that he had found one, but when he showed it to me, I was quite unable to see it. I managed to grin and make agreeable noises. We then saddled the horses and started off. On foot it might not have been so bad, but huge charred tree-trunks lay everywhere and it was almost impossible to get the horses over them, their energy greatly depleted since they had failed to find any food during the night. We struggled along until dusk, having covered perhaps another two miles, and by this time Hernandez was in despair.

"This is impossible. We have no food, the horses will starve and we cannot get them out of here. Tomorrow the launch will come, and we must make smoke signals for Mr. Williams." I felt furious but, as one of the horses was his, and he was also responsible to Mr. Bridges for the other, I could not honestly blame him, although I had a sneaking feeling that, had I been with Ramon Dias, it would have been a very different story. But there could be no doubt about the impossibility of obtaining food; neither was there, I could see, anything for the horses. If only we could have gone on farther, it might not have been so bad, but as it was we were forced to return over much of the way we had so laboriously come, to reach a small, rocky promontory that had a little beach on one side from which it would be easy to get the horses into the water.

By this time we were both so exhausted that the fact of also having no food seemed hardly to matter any more. We made a strong cup of coffee and finished the evaporated milk. Heartened by this refreshment, I staggered up to the top of the rocky point and saw to my disgust the glow of a camp fire that looked not much farther off than the point at which we had turned back. We stayed near the water and early next morning were out gathering fire-wood for the three smokes. We got the horses ready on the beach, and I went up to the promontory to watch for the *Andes* while Hernandez stood ready below to light the three fires. At last I saw a plume of smoke far out on the lake and called to him. In no time, three large clouds of smoke rose up in the sky. I ran down ready to drive the horses into the water. Hernandez was smiling and grinning, but, to our horror, we soon noticed that there was no sign of change in the *Andes'* course, nor friendly toots from her motor, and it began to dawn on us that our wonderful smokes had not been seen. Hernandez became frantic, and I was torn between a certain satisfaction that we should now be obliged to go on and disappointment that I should be unable to satisfy my gnawing hunger. For the next few minutes we tried with quite futile cries to attract the attention of the launch as we drove the horses up and down the little beach, hoping this movement on a deserted shore might be noticed, but the *Andes* chugged placidly away and disappeared round the next point.

All hope of retreat now absolutely lost, Hernandez seemed to pull himself together, and we decided to leave the horses and try to reach the point at which I had seen the fire the night before. We struck off through the charred forest, but even without the horses it was not easy, and night had fallen by the time, exhausted and starving, we caught sight of the fire glowing quite near through the trees.

We came to a small clearing roughly fenced in and a sort of three-sided "lean-to", roofed with small branches and moss. In front of its open side the fire was burning — a huge log about 15 feet long and three feet in diameter with sticks leaning against it gradually burning a hollow in the centre, the two smouldering ends serving as a sort of self-igniting fire-place. Over the fire hung a large iron pot and stirring it with a long wooden ladle was a young woman, a baby on her hip. She looked up when she heard the noise of our approach and her calm, beautiful face seemed to be looking at me out of a Renaissance Madonna painting. Like a Madonna she smiled a gentle welcome, indicating the end of the log with a bend of her head, and said quietly, "You are tired, please sit down." She ladled a thick white mixture out of the iron pot into a small wooden bowl and, handing it to me, said, "You must be hungry, eat." She then served Hernandez and, while we thankfully gobbled down the delicious porridge, she sat silently watching us.

Hungry as I was I could not help staring at her. Perhaps it was because of my exhaustion that she made such an impression on me, but never before or since have I seen a human being who transmitted such an atmosphere of goodness and peace. Even the baby was good and, as the warmth and food worked its customary magic, I began to notice other figures round the fire, about six children, staring — like wild things of the forest — at us, until out of the darkness and into the firelight swept the patriarch himself, Don Acuna, father of the tribe and husband of the Madonna. At the age of almost 70, he had made his third expedition to Chiloe and brought her back as his third wife. I did not like to enquire what had happened to the first two wives, but there were the six children to prove that they had lingered a few years at least.

Don Acuna was graciousness itself. "You will stay the night in my house," he said, on hearing of our troubles and waving towards the lean-to with a gesture worthy of a castle. "In the morning I will send my peon to help you bring the horses in. Now is the time for sleep." I looked round at the children rather apprehensively as I had not been able to bring my sleeping bag with me and should certainly be obliged to share a bed with one or more of the girls. Even in the dim firelight they looked quite remarkably dirty. I had not done much washing myself lately, it is true, but whenever I got the chance I always had a dab, while these people could never have washed, and it was really providential that the annual rainfall in Patagonia is so enormous.

Don Acuna shepherded us all towards the shed and then disappeared behind it with Hernandez. After a certain amount of polite argument, I got on to one of the simple raft-like beds of plain planks nailed together flat on the ground, with two little girls of about seven and five, a lovely woolly puppy and an enormous grey cat — quite the cleanest of us all.

We were up early in the morning, but by the time we had had more porridge and coffee and Don Acuna had found two axes, it was nearly nine. Just as we were leaving with two of the elder boys, Don Acuna gave a loud shout, answered by a high-pitched shriek, and round the fence came a strange newcomer. It was an elderly man, entirely bald except for one tuft of hair which had grown to a foot in length. It hung down his back and a few strands came forward to mingle with a large bushy beard. In his hand he held a dirty white beret. He was introduced as El Espagñol, and he was the peon. We all followed the trail that Hernandez and I had so laboriously made the day before, but we got back a good deal faster than we had come. The horses, poor things, after two days without food were very easy to catch and saddle. The sleeping bag and our few clothes were divided between myself and the two boys, leaving Hernandez and the peon to wield the axes.

At first our prospects of making headway seemed poor. The horses had to get up a narrow cliff and then traverse the stone face on a slippery little track about 15 inches wide. The peon stood at the point where the muddy track began while we urged the horses up the cliff-side from below. The first one made it alright, but the second fell backwards down the cliff. We got it up on its feet and, to my astonishment, it was quite unhurt but naturally refused to make another attempt, and we had to make its life unbearable below so that it finally tried again and this time succeeded. Our progress then became a walking nightmare. The men chopped and cut at the deadfalls with their axes, the boys and I tried to clear away the fallen branches but, in the end, we still had to depend on luck. Hernandez would contemplate the so-called cleared section, look mournfully at me, as I held the horses ready, shake his head and say, "If they are lamed, they are lamed, no more." Then I would let them go and the boys would beat them behind to try and rouse them enough to jump all the obstacles we had not been able to clear away. After three hours we came to a bog on the edge of a precipice out of which gnarled roots of long-dead trees were sticking, creating an additional hazard that we could do nothing about. When at last we got the horses across, we came not only to a comparatively easy track but, wonder of wonders, to a good piece of pasture land, and so decided to leave them there for the night.

We got back to the Acunas' and found more lovely porridge cooking slowly over the fire, and Don Acuna told me tall stories about the fine farm he had once owned. "And now look at me, condemned to live here in hiding!" I felt it might be a breach of good manners to ask the reason of so hospitable a host.

In the morning Hernandez and I went back to fetch the horses and then, after an *asado*, Don Acuna accompanying us, we rode to the top of a pass leading to another arm of the lake. Here Don Acuna left us and we rode on down, camping that evening in a damp, dismal place, redeemed by some fair grazing, and the next morning continued to the point where Rio Leone joins the lake. Hernandez was becoming increasingly gloomy with every step. He had avidly absorbed El Espagñol's tales about the difficulties of crossing it. Apparently it was unusually deep, extremely fast and could only be crossed in one point and then only in the early morning.

When we got to the river's edge, however, things brightened up. There was a house and in it lived a man with eight daughters. He said he would be glad to guide us over if I could take a photograph of his eight daughters, for he was, not unnaturally, very proud of them. The eldest, just 14, was now of marriageable age, and there was about a year between each of the girls. As every prospective husband would give him a nice present in cash, he could now look forward to at least eight carefree years. He led us through the river very efficiently but, as we zigzagged our horses chest-deep through the opaque water, it seemed a miracle that he himself had ever found his way over in the first place, and his warnings seemed to crush Hernandez' spirits.

"You will have to be very careful, as you have only two horses," we were told. "Even one day's rain is enough to kill a horse. The last people I took across this river took 12 days to do 50 miles, and for four days their horses got no food."

Watching Hernandez' face as this saga unfolded, I could see that nothing would induce him to take the horses along, but I was determined to let him broach the subject first. Luckily, however, after we left the river, the weather remained fair, and late in the afternoon we found a wonderful pasture where we decided to camp in order to let the horses stuff themselves against the rigors to come. Unfortunately, it began to rain while we were making a nauseating stew of all our left-overs. We were glumly eating it when Hernandez announced that he would go no farther.

"But what else can you do?" I asked, for which he found no answer, and as we crouched disputatiously over the fire, the owner of the pasture rode up. We turned to him in our trouble and he quickly settled our problems.

"In five days a boat is coming for some of my cows to take them across the lake, and you," turning to Hernandez, "can go with them. The Señorita can take one of my horses and go 12 miles to the house of a man with a rowing-boat. He will take her up to the *muette*, where there is another man who could hire her a horse to come down the other side."

I agreed heartily with this suggestion, although I had not of course the least idea what a *muette* was. At least it meant that I would be able to continue my travels and not return, defeated, with Hernandez.

CHAPTER EIGHT
THE END OF THE RIDE

VERY early in the morning we were at the house of the pasture-owner, where I bade Hernandez a thankful farewell, realising that he was every bit as glad to see the last of me as I of him. The horse I was given to ride on the next stage of my journey to the house of Don Juan, owner of the rowing-boat, looked quite a reasonable animal, and when I heard that he also belonged to Don Juan, I felt more confident of eventually arriving. I could not help feeling a little like Alice in Wonderland as I rode away on a track that seemed easy to follow but after a couple of miles led into another area devastated by fire.

It was the most dismal scenery that I have ever seen. The horse's hooves sank inches deep into the grey ash that covered the ground and occasionally he went in up to the knee; there were enormous dead trees with broken, blackened branches hanging despairingly down over a crisscross of charred trunks lying on the ground. Both rider and horse became slowly coated with fine grey ash, and the track was now obliterated, but the horse went slowly forward, and I supposed he knew where he was going. Every now and then we would pass a stump that stuck out of the ash, still sending up a plume of smoke. After a couple of hours of this, my nerves, already on edge, received another shock. A strangled cry broke the uncanny silence. The start I gave nearly cost me my seat. The cry came again, and looking apprehensively round, I saw a pathetic group of sheep that had, by a miracle, survived the fire but were now slowly dying of starvation. It was remarkable that they had survived at all, but there could be little hope of their lasting much longer because the thin soil had been burnt away, as well as the trees, and under the ash lay naked rock, gradually exposed as the rain washed this grey coating away.

Thinking of the harsh cruelty of this beautiful country, I began to wonder if the desolate ride would ever end. Then I saw smoke rising up through the burnt trees and, as I got nearer, found it issuing from a small shack. A young man appeared, Don Juan himself, and was very pleased to see the horse that had been borrowed two weeks before.

He invited me in, and no sooner had I got inside and was peering through the smoke that was always a permanent feature of this type of chimney-less dwelling, than my arm was clutched, and a shrill female voice demanded that I come and look at her daughter's leg.

I was led by a wizened old woman to a heap of blankets on which lay a girl of about 14. Her left leg was wrapped in a filthy bandage, which the old woman removed, disclosing a very large, angry-looking boil covered by a cabbage leaf. I gazed at it and suggested hot-water compresses, changed constantly, but the old lady, looking absolutely disgusted, said, "I had a friend who did that for her boil and she burnt her leg so badly that she was crippled for life." She then seized another large cabbage leaf from the floor and clapped it over the boil.

Since there was obviously no more I could do in a medical way, I explained — or tried to explain (for I had very little idea myself) — where I wanted to go, and there were the usual responses of, *"Como no?"* Don Juan said he was taking the boat but gave no hint of his destination. Tomorrow I could go with him. As we sat talking, a man came in with a barrel of wine, and a few minutes later a boy. To each of these, the old woman showed her daughter's leg, and each time rejected any proffered advice on similar grounds. She had had a friend who had tried this or that but had been permanently handicapped as a result. The daughter said nothing. The boil might not have belonged to her at all.

There were no beds in the house, for which I felt thankful, since this meant that I could sleep by myself, but it was a depressing evening. I began to think that there was some justification for Ramon Diaz' opinion of the Chileans. Across the other side of the lake, in the Argentine, men rode across open spaces and, when hungry, killed a sheep and roasted it under the wide sky. These people crouched round a smoking fire in a shack huddled under large trees cutting off all the view of a sky that intermittently deluged them with rain. They all had an air of having given up. Life had become too much for them. They had absolutely nothing — not even religion — to give point to their lives.

In the morning the man and boy, who had come the evening before, loaded me, my saddle and the barrel of wine, into a small leaky rowing-boat. We rowed for about two miles downstream and anchored in a little bay. Here we unloaded and carried everything up a hill where some other settlers were having a *trecia*. This was the reason for the barrel of wine. The harvest, which was minute, had already been threshed, so the drinking was seriously under way. Quite soon after the arrival of our barrel, everybody was drunk except for one solitary woman, to whom the man had handed me over rather as though I were a parcel, saying he could take me no farther but that she and her husband would take me to their house where a man with a *trupilla* was rumoured to be passing next morning. The woman said she would be glad to take me in and send me to a point where I might meet the *trupilla*. Again, no mention of destination, and just as I had myself given up saying where I wanted to go, neither did anyone ever ask me. They took for granted that so long as I was going somewhere I should be all right. They were not far wrong; as long as I was not obliged to retrace my steps, I was quite happy and by the time that the woman, Señora Monte, and I had come to this agreement, the rest of the company had reached the comatose stage, and she began walking round among the prostrate bodies looking for her husband.

Finally she selected one figure and started to hoist it to its feet. I went to help her. He was a large man, very good-natured and, I decided, not nearly as drunk as he pretended because just as soon as we got him to the boat, he stepped in, smartly, unaided, sat down on the middle thwart, with me facing him in the stern and his wife in the bow, and started rowing away. As he rowed he would now and again give me a huge wink, pulling up his shirt to show me a bottle of wine tucked in the top of his trousers. When we got to the house, it was surprisingly smart, having two windows and a door. The husband, no sooner freed from the rigors of rowing, subsided at once on a bench with his bottle and, by the time the Señora and I had eaten some warmed-up *puchero*, had fallen unconscious on the floor. I went outside to fetch my bedding and on returning, found the Señora had opened the store-room door with an enormous key and was insisting that I spend the night locked inside it because, she said, it would be "*Muy seguro.*"

In the morning the husband was nowhere to be seen, but the Señora told me she had a horse ready for me to ride to the spot where the *trupilla* was expected to pass. A peon would go with me to show the way and bring the horse back. The peon was a small, dark man, a half-breed Indian, and as we rode in silence through the dreadful devastation of the fire, the ash enveloped us in a grisly pall, seeping into our clothes and up our nostrils as we breathed and into our mouths if we opened them.

After about five or six hours of this, we came to a miserable shack where there was a woman with five children. She told us that the *trupilla* had not yet passed and that I could stay with her until it came. The poor thing was nearly demented with strain and grief and talked without stopping. Her second son had been drowned in the river two days before and her eldest son burnt to death in the forest fire. Inside the shack was her father with a huge open wound on his leg from a burn he had got at the same time as his grandson had died. The grandfather was only alive because he had found a small pool of water in which he lay while the fire burnt all round him.

The rest of the children had been in the house with their mother, but the fire advanced so fast that in 15 minutes it had spread six miles. They had all rushed out of the house but had had no time to take anything with them. They had run down into the river and spent the whole day sitting in water up to their necks until the fire had burnt itself out. The house she was now in was the best her husband had been able to fix up before he left for Chiloe, where he hoped to get some work, but as it was already autumn, his chances did not look too bright.

While she was telling me all this, one of the younger children came in with some puff balls. These she broke open very carefully and sprinkled the powder over the old man's wound, saying, "Spiders' webs are really better but even all the spiders were burnt."

These awful happenings brought home to me again the terrible difficulties that these poor women faced. With two or three children they could probably manage to make some sort of a home, but with each additional child, things became more and more difficult until finally they were living in conditions worse than any animal's. In a country where they could have had a mother or sister to help, it would not have been so bad, but here, where even the nearest neighbour could be living at least five hours' ride away and might not even own a house, this was out of the question. I never saw a grandmother during my entire ride, and never more than one adult woman in any house, no matter how many children there were. As all the men seemed to have been married at least three times, it obviously meant that the mortality was very high indeed among the women of child-bearing age, and I hardly saw one above this age. These conditions never prevailed on any of the large *estancias*.

While I waited, hopefully, for the arrival of the *trupilla*, I wrestled with my conscience to decide how much money I could offer the poor woman. Clothes would have been a far more practical gift, but I had literally nothing but what I was wearing and, as the weather was getting colder day by day, I could not bring myself to give my shirt away. I had no means of judging how much longer it might take as to reach Puerto Aysen, which would be the first place where I should be able to get more money, and I should certainly need some even to get me there.

While I was wrestling with the problem, I heard the sound of hooves, and rushing out, saw — to me like an angel from heaven — a young half-breed called Pedro, with no less than seven horses, pulling up by the house. I asked him whether he could take me on. *"Como no?"* was his cheerful response, and when I asked him what he would charge me, he said, "It is not far to where you can get a boat, two days, no more. I am going with these horses anyway, so why should you pay anything?"

Overcome with this generosity, I immediately doubled the sum I had decided to give the woman of the house, and when I pressed it into her hand, expressing my thanks, it was a sure measure of her need that she took it, quite simply, without a word of protest.

I fetched my saddle, and we caught one of the *trupilla* and saddled it, then rode off in the pouring rain for Pedro's house. He had just got married and was full of enthusiasm over his bride. "Wait till you see her, she is beautiful! Five thousand pesos I paid for her!"

After a few hours' ride we came to his house, a one-roomed shack with a dirt floor turned by every downpour rain into mud. A wood fire was burning in the centre of the floor raised above the mud on stones. The bride, an enormously fat Indian girl, staggered to greet us in a pair of high-heeled patent leather shoes. She made me very welcome, and as we crouched on sections of tree-trunks ranged round the fire, I watched the smoke trying to get out of the door while the rain tried to get in. The rain seemed to be winning. Pedro discussed the dreadful poverty of the woman whose house I had just left.

"Poor thing! She has no capital, without capital life is not possible, is that not so?" I earnestly agreed.

The rain continued without let or pause until there was no dry spot on the floor, by which time we were all ready to go to bed. Pedro and his wife had a double-bed rigged up on a tarpaulin, but there was some discussion as to where I could go. Finally we made a raised platform with some planks of wood and the slices of tree-trunks, and under my waterproof poncho *castilla*, I spent a fairly comfortable night, but by morning there was no improvement in the weather and it was in low spirits that I started out after Pedro.

All my worst fears were fulfilled. The way was hideous, the horses either slithering down steep barrancas or slipping backwards down them. Even Pedro's high spirits began to flag, and he murmured that perhaps we could not ride to the place he had in mind and it might be better to go to another place where there was a boat. We could take that, he said, and try to swim the horses across the *muette*, which I was now coming to realise must be a kind of bay. We slipped and staggered out of the forest, coming to a small shed at the water's edge. Through the rain I could just see a long row of hills on the other side of the *muette*. There was a man asleep in the shed and, after waking him and exchanging all the usual courtesies, we saw the rain suddenly stop like a tap being turned off and a furious wind spring up that put all further thoughts of a boat out of our minds, and we got back on our horses and plodded on.

We soon found ourselves in dense virgin forest, far from all signs of the fire. Huge trees towered high overhead, draped with creepers, but underfoot was bog. At the first patch of dry ground we lay down to spend the night. We did not sleep well and at daybreak were thankful to get up and start off again.

Towards three o'clock in the afternoon we came to another shack, the owner of which had two boats and said he would be glad to take me across the bay, but we should have to stay the night, as it was still far too rough for his boats. He added, with what I considered to be unnecessary relish, that it could easily blow like this for four days on end.

While we were standing there, gloomily contemplating the water, a man called out: *"El Andes! El Andes!"*, and, sure enough, there she was, squat and dirty, but an answer to my prayers. We ran onto the beach, furiously collecting firewood. Pedro lit three piles with miraculous ease, considering that the wood was soaking wet, but they sent up splendid smoke signals, and the woman of the house now came running with dirty towels to wave as well. This time the *Andes* saw us. She altered course and slowed down, coming in as close as she could to the shore, and there was Mr. Williams, laughing and waving from the bridge as we rowed out. Ten minutes later I was sitting in the warm saloon, a big mug of coffee in my hands, talking to him.

"Well, you didn't do so badly," he grinned. "I never thought you would get as far as this. I saw Hernandez and he was convinced you had gone to your death."

The *Andes* was going up to the head of the *muette* for firewood. That suited me splendidly, and I decided to stay with her until I could find another *trupilla* going north. The man who cut the fuel for the *Andes* lived with his wife in a small hovel on the cliff above a beach stacked with firewood. Mr. Williams asked me to go up there and get the woman to sell me one of her chickens. We could see about 20 of them scratching round the house. I walked up the muddy track to the door, and a small girl of about nine emerged with three smaller children in tow. They all regarded me solemnly. "Is your mother in?" I asked.

"In bed with the baby," she replied.

I was not quite sure what to do and, as I hesitated, a voice inside called, and the eldest child disappeared, leaving the other three staring silently at me. When she reappeared she said, "Mother asks you to come in."

Inside I was assailed by the usual dense cloud of smoke but managed to discover, lying beneath a pile of grubby blankets, an exhausted-looking woman with enormous eyes. "Please sit down," she murmured in a weak voice.

"I've come from the *Andes*," I said. The woman knew Mr. Williams and said that her husband had now been away for three weeks, then lay back exhausted, closing her eyes. As the children had followed me in, I turned to the eldest and said, "Your mother looks so ill, is there anything I could do?"

She shook her head. "It is the baby. He was born three days ago, and she has not felt well since."

"Have you enough to eat?"

"Yes, we have smoked meat and we do not need to cook it."

"But perhaps it would do your mother good to have something hot. What about killing one of the hens and I could cook it for you?"

The child was horrified. "Oh no! The hens belong to someone else, and we are only looking after them. Our cows are at pasture 20 miles away."

A wail from the bed interrupted this conversation and roused the mother. She moved the corner of a dirty blanket and pulled a little wizened baby towards her to suckle. I murmured a hurried goodbye and went into the good fresh air and returned to report to Mr. Williams. He was quite unimpressed by my description of the family but very dashed to learn that the hens were not for sale. He looked at my anxious face and said, "Don't worry over it. There is nothing you can do. I should never have a moment's peace if I paid any attention to the lives of these people who live round here. You must just learn to shut your mind to it."

He had brought a piece of meat ashore with him, so we sat down and lit a fire to make an *asado*. While we were waiting for it to cook, he said he would be crossing the *muette* early next morning and could introduce me to a Señor Urutia, who owned several horses and might easily be able to take me on to the Fugellies. By the time we finished our *asado*, the firewood was all loaded on the *Andes*, so we went back on board and turned in, and it seemed wonderful to be neither wet nor choked with smoke nor yet to share my bunk with a very grubby fellow human.

The next day I met Señor Urutia, a tiny man with a wrinkled face like a little monkey. He lived alone in a small, neat house and said he would be delighted to take me to the Fugellies, as he was leaving in any case to take his *trupilla* down for better grazing near their *estancia* and was only waiting for a Don Juan, who had been in the interior with a Chilean engineer prospecting for another route through the Cordillera that would reach Puerto Aysen without passing in and out of Argentine territory.

After spending another night on the *Andes*, I landed the next morning with my saddle and walked to Señor Urutia's house. Don Juan had arrived the evening before and was a most impressive figure in high-heeled boots and jangling spurs. White goat-skin chaps encased his legs, and he wore a poncho and black sombrero, which he swept off, raising my hand gallantly to his lips. "With your company, the journey will now be a true pleasure," he assured me gravely. Señor Urutia now came round with a long-backed brown horse which he said was for me. Don Juan's was black, to match his clothes.

As soon as my horse was saddled, we went to the paddock to join the *trupilla*. Señor Urutia had to lead his horse to a large stump so that he could mount, and, when mounted, looked more like a dear little monkey than ever, his short legs ending in tiny boots that seemed to dangle just over the edge of his saddle, but he was a superb horseman. Possibly because he was so small that mounting and dismounting presented such difficulty, at any rate he rode nonchalantly over the most extraordinary country, consisting almost entirely of precipices or huge boulders. But, fortunately for me, Don Juan was not at all of like calibre and was always as ready as I was to dismount at the dangerous-looking places. Señor Urutia, when he reached the top or bottom of some, to me, unnegotiable place, would turn to contemplate us, toiling away on foot, quite often on all fours, and murmur softly, "You find it steep, Don Juan?"

The long-backed brown horse was an excellent mount, taking the steepest hill without changing his stride, and it was with real regret that I said goodbye to all of them at the end of the second day when we reached the Fugellies, an English family: husband, wife and two teenaged daughters.

Mrs. Fugellie had come out as a nurse to an English family and had met and married her husband in Patagonia. They had settled on land off the northern shore of Lake Buenos Aires, and with no capital whatever, had made a wonderful success of it. The house was well built of wood, painted, and with a good chimney. They kept cows, hens and a vegetable garden. After all the sordid places I had been seeing, it was like a breath of fresh air to see what people with imagination and diligence could accomplish. They had had no more to start with than most of the families on the other side of the lake, but the difference in achievement had to be seen to be believed. We enjoyed three good meals a day, with snacks in between, and there was plenty of variety. After my diet of *puchero*, the milk, butter and cream were what appealed to me most.

The only means of communication was by the *Andes* in summer, or on horseback, taking two and a half days to Puerto Aysen. This meant that anything not produced on the place represented considerable value, and on my second day there, a major catastrophe occurred. The china teapot broke. We all crawled on the floor looking for pieces. There were four big pieces and six small ones, but we found them all. For the next hour, the two girls were piecing them carefully together, tying them with string to hold them in place till the whole teapot was enclosed in string netting. They then put it carefully on the dresser and waited until the evening milking was done, when they poured about four gallons of milk into a large iron pot in which they stood the broken teapot. They lit a fire under it and set the milk on the boil for four hours, adding more milk as soon as the teapot became uncovered. After four hours it was left to cool and, when next morning the string was removed, the pot was mended and we had our tea out of it as usual.

Puerto Aysen now being my objective, I was glad to learn that I could catch a lorry there which would take me across to Comodoro Rivadavia on the Atlantic coast; from there it would be easy to get to Buenos Aires. One day an Indian and his son came across from cutting wood on one of the islands. They said they were going back to Puerto Aysen and I could travel with them. The son would bring back my horse when he returned. When we set off at daybreak it soon became plain that neither was a keen horseman.

They seized every opportunity to walk, an example that I was not slow to follow. My horse, a black, was small, thin and weak. I felt guilty when I thought of what he had to carry. Besides myself in the huge black poncho, he carried my heavy Australian saddle, two sheepskins, a large piece of waterproof canvas, and my gear in a cotton saddlebag. However, the poor beast got me to Puerto Aysen and naturally gave me no trouble when I was catching him every morning.

After all the rain, I had almost forgotten that there was such a thing as good weather and, to my surprise, the sun shone during the whole of our first day, so that I was warm and comfortable in a shirt, but that night it froze hard. The next day a piercing wind blew in our faces, and it seemed as though the day would never end. José, the father, was almost crippled by his rheumatism, and we were all thankful when we came to a sheltered wood and could get a fire going. As soon as our *asado* began to sizzle in front of it and we could enjoy the warmth and shelter, life felt perfect again.

We had now reached the region where the Chileans were building a motor-road. As the Argentines charged duty on any goods in transit for Puerto Aysen, it was absolutely imperative for the Chileans to have a road running along their side of the border. Work on it had already begun. Coming down the northern slope of the pass, it appeared to me as though the road were going to run alongside the winding river, but at the moment, it merely descended to the river-bed itself. When our horses were not moving along the river-bed, they were knee-deep in a bog to one side of it. We crawled along at a funeral pace, poor José gradually getting stiffer and stiffer. It made me ache all over to see him dismount. We finally came to some better going where some men were working on the road, and we jogged along happily, believing our troubles to be at an end, until we reached a spot where men were blasting a path between cliff-face and river.

It appeared to be merely a stretch of 20 yards of deep, black mud without any possible alternative trail, and while our unfortunate animals floundered through it, the workmen on the cliff above watched our laborious progress with evident enjoyment. As we reached firm ground, surfaced with sharp flints so that our unshod horses had to pick their way gingerly, we met a boy who came running round a corner and collided into us. He went, of course, through all the routine courtesies without which it is considered rude to start any conversation, and then said quietly, "You must turn back because of the blasting." Even as he spoke, there was a deafening detonation that startled even our tired animals into instant action, and showers of stones fell all round us, luckily none large enough to do much damage. Two more explosions followed, after which the road-makers seemed to have no more to offer us. We camped for the night in a small wood, and next morning José said that we must really get to Aysen even if it meant riding all night.

We jogged all day along a dull road, while my spirits slowly sank as the prospect of reaching civilisation drew nearer. I could not stop myself speculating about the future which, after months of adhering to the motto: "Sufficient unto the day are the evils thereof," I found terribly tiring.

It looked as though José was going to be right about riding all night. As dusk fell there was no sign of any houses, and we kept going in the pitch darkness, the horses having some difficulty finding their way, until at last we saw the lights of a house and decided it would be better to stop and camp in a field nearby. Without troubling to light a fire or to cook, we lay down and fell asleep, completely exhausted. In the morning, when I woke up, my hair was frozen to my poncho. After I had released myself, I was surprised to find that we had actually arrived and were camping out in the heart of the town.

Aysen was a pretty little place when it could be seen without rain, but in the two days that I was there, we had barely two hours of sunshine. These two days were amongst the longest in my life. The so-called hotel was unbelievably cold and if it had not been for the mussels — two inches long and pure heaven — that we had for dinner each night, I should certainly have gone mad. Acute discomfort in forest or desert is one thing, but the depression of a sleazy, ill-heated, verminous hotel, is quite something else.

CHAPTER NINE
MARRIAGE

R ETURNING to civilisation from primitive conditions always saddens me. Its worst aspects come first. I started with the hotel in Aysen whose plumbing arrangements made a bush on the pampas a thing to look back on with envy. Then came the lorry drive along the so-called "road" to Comodoro Rivadavia; it was hard to tell which was in worse condition, the lorry or the road.

Decisions had to be made and dates fixed for passages on boats and aircraft. After months of living by chance happenings with no idea of time, I needed to readjust to a new way of life. I felt relieved when I was on the boat at last in Buenos Aires, where for the next fortnight I could not possibly change the course of events.

I had had letters from Miles. He was in England on leave from India and would have three weeks left by the time I arrived there. As soon as I knew myself, I had written telling him when I was leaving Buenos Aires and by what boat, so as we approached Cherbourg I was wondering if he might be there. The ship drew alongside and among the waiting figures was one head and shoulders taller than the rest. He had come to Cherbourg to meet me.

I did not have much luggage and was soon on the quay, then we were in a café. Time slipped away unnoticed as we talked, laughed and forgot that we had ever been separated. Surprisingly, he still wanted to marry me. It was queer how in two years of constant separation neither of us could take a fancy to anyone else.

The day was lovely, a perfect European spring, and our thoughts were the same; we must get away from the town and into the country. We wanted to be on our own; not tied down by timetables of buses or trains. As we were both short of money, bicycles were the perfect answer. We spent a happy hour in a bicycle shop trying various bikes, and in the proprietor's little workshop sorting out our clothes so as to take the least possible. In the early afternoon we pedalled out of Cherbourg, in the French fashion, with our heads well down and our behinds well up.

For the next week we bicycled slowly round the Caen Peninsula. The weather, joining in our happiness, only gave us one rainy day, and the French people fully lived up to their reputation for loving lovers. Always when I think of those golden days, I hear the song: "Look down, look down that lonely road before you travel on." This was what Miles considered his winning trump, and he would always sing it after we had been talking about getting married. It may have worked on me subconsciously, as I had known for some time that I could not marry anybody else while I loved him, so by the time we left for England we had decided to get married.

We took a bus at Victoria Station straight from the boat-train for Caxton Hall Registry Office. Miles bought a paper and immersed himself in it; the bus sailed past the Registry Office, and the man who had been asking me to marry him so ardently for over two

Beryl.

years let it pass. I was a bit nonplussed and when we reached Westminster Abbey, joined in, rather falsely, with his laughter over not noticing. We caught the next bus back. Again no move from Miles until the bus came to rest in Victoria Station. This time he had the grace to look a little ashamed. Our third attempt was successful, chiefly due, I think, to the fact that he had finished the interesting part of the paper. Inside the office, the clerk, on being asked, said it would be impossible to marry us under three weeks, as we neither of us had resided in London. There was no way round; one of us had to be resident somewhere. Miles now became very keen and, on the clerk's suggestion, rang up the Registry Office in Malton, the town in Yorkshire near his home. There they were very cheerful and accommodating. A male voice, in broad Yorkshire, said over the phone that if we could get there by 8:30 on Monday morning they would "Put t'harness on properly."

It was now lunchtime Saturday, and although there was no real hurry, when faced with these difficulties we were both seized with a passionate desire to be married on Monday morning at 8:30. So we rushed off to Waterloo Station and took a train down to my brother's house in Dorset where I had left my Baby Austin car. We spent that night with Charles, and Miles sent off a telegram to a friend he had planned to go climbing with, explaining that we were getting married and asking if I could come too. Then at dawn on Sunday we started off for Yorkshire.

We were the first clients at the Malton Registry Office at 8:30 on Monday morning and found that we now needed witnesses, so we had to go out in the town to solicit help from passers-by. At that hour there were few people on the streets. Miles told me to go left and he would go right. My side was absolutely bare except for the butcher's shop, which was open. I went in and stood waiting. The butcher was wrapping up some meat for a customer and, as he handed it across, he turned to me saying, "What can I do for you, Madam?"

"Please could you be a witness at my wedding?"

"Why certainly," he replied with great aplomb. "Just a second and I'll wash my hands."

He gave them a perfunctory rinse under the tap, stuck his carving knife in the belt of his apron, and came round the counter to accompany me across the road. Miles was already back with a very gloomy individual wearing a bowler hat and bicycle clips.

As soon as the introductions were over, the butcher took charge of the social side of the proceedings, keeping up a jolly commentary, as: "If I had known how easy it was I'd have been married years ago," while the Registrar completed his forms. When we had paid and filed outside, he gave Miles' hand a crushing grip and said, "My heartiest congratulations, you're a lucky man, Sir." He then took my hand and bowed very low over it, saying, "Best of luck to you, Madam."

The gloomy man now felt he should say something and diffidently began to congratulate me but was stopped instantly by the butcher who said, "You must never congratulate the bride, it's luck they need."

It was not perhaps very much of a wedding, but it was at least entirely ours. We had done it all ourselves to suit ourselves, and we had enjoyed it. The butcher with his apt remarks gave a festive air to the proceedings, and the gloomy man served to remind us that "Life is real, life is earnest," a fact we were in danger of forgetting.

Afterwards we drove round and broke our news to Miles' astonished, and sometimes dismayed, relatives. At his mother's house was the answer to Miles' telegram to Bill: "Delighted congratulations," it said, "am bringing Mother and trailer too."

We had had so many uncertain partings that when it came time for Miles to leave we had no sense of loss. We were married now and in about another six weeks I would be arriving in Bombay.

"I'll get leave and come down and meet you," said Miles. "Have a good time with Elsie."

Elsie was an old family friend of the Smeetons, well on in her 60s and a real English eccentric. She lived in a house filled with Siamese cats, and in the garden she kept a pet pig. She was gentle and frail-looking, with a backbone of steel and, as I was to find out later, quite deaf to any mechanical noise made by a car. She had become a Moslem, and when we had gone to see her after our wedding, she was talking about going to Egypt.

"Why don't you drive out there with Beryl?" Miles said lightheartedly. "She is driving there in the Baby Austin and will put it on the *Lloyd Triestina* in Port Said."

Elsie was absolutely delighted with the idea, so I found myself, rather unexpectedly, with a passenger. I planned to drive to Marseilles, take a boat from there to Algiers, then motor along the North African coast to Cairo, camping out where possible on the way.

96

I wanted to start as soon as possible, and when I saw the Automobile Association about getting the necessary papers and permits, I realised that if I changed over to my married name it would take at least two weeks more, so I carried on as Miss Boxer. The Automobile Association's account of what we might expect to meet along the North African coast made me take a few lessons in car maintenance, and in a burst of enthusiasm I learnt to service the Austin, going so far as to even decarbonise it.

The journey was in complete contrast to the Patagonian one. This time I was only travelling to arrive. The actual journey was not my main interest. It was also done with mechanical transport. I was passing through other countries entirely self-sufficient; my car proclaimed me to be an outsider, and I could only look in from the outside. I think also it was harder to make friends with people because there were two of us. Sometimes in the villages people might, seeing me alone and thinking me to be lonely, have struck up a conversation, but with two of us they were not nearly so likely to think of it. As we passed through countries which were so rich in recorded history, I felt I was missing the most important part. I got no real feel of the people themselves and their thoughts.

Nearly all the journeys I have made I have slightly marred by trying to travel too quickly, and this one I pushed on even faster as I was wanting to get out and see Miles. But once we arrived in Africa and had left the city of Algiers behind and camped our first night under the young moon, out of sight of any human habitation with only the road stretching before us, I felt for the first time since leaving England a feeling of release.

The roads in Algeria, at least outside the towns, were dirt. They were well-graded and broad, being, I suppose, mostly strategic. We soon found that the best way to travel in the intense heat, for it was now July, was to start at about four a.m. and drive till ten a.m. Then we would stop just off the road and unroll the canvas cover attached to the roof of the car and sit and doze in its shade till the early afternoon, when we would start again.

We made various little detours off the main road to see any ruins we thought might be interesting, and one day as we were on our way to see what was supposed to be a particularly fine amphitheatre, Elsie said we must stop as she had diarrhea. We progressed after that in fits and starts, so when we got to the little town near the amphitheatre I was thankful to find that it had a small hotel where we could stay the night. It was not much of an hotel and hardly reassuring to anyone suffering from suspected dysentery, being filled with flies and possessing a lavatory that functioned in a very Gallic way. However, the beds were excellent, and as soon as she was lying down with a bottle of Vichy water beside her, Elsie said she felt so much better that she urged me to go out and see the ruins.

I drove off and soon found myself jammed in one of the narrow streets of the native city, with several donkeys pressing up behind while some camels regarded me disgustedly from the front. Various Arabs sprang up shouting and gesticulating, but until the animals moved there was nothing much I could do, so I sat tight. Suddenly, to my great relief, I heard an English voice saying, "You seem to be in need of a bit of help." I craned my head out of the car and saw a young Foreign Legionnaire standing beside it.

"Well, I was looking for the ruins."

"They are not far. I'll come and show you," he said, opening the door and getting in. The crowd had fallen silent while we were talking, so he seized the opportunity and, speaking in fluent Arabic, soon found who were the owners of the various animals and got them under control while I moved the car on. The ruins were not far away, on higher ground than the present town, and although they were quite uncared for, their size and grandeur were to me more fascinating than the restored and refurbished ones I was to see later in Mussolini's Africa. We must have wandered round looking for nearly an hour, but I was so taken by the idea of actually meeting a Foreign Legionnaire that I found myself paying more attention to him than to the ruins.

Well primed by various novels I had read and films I had seen, I was careful not to ask him too many personal questions, but he told me what I had already guessed from his accent, that he was of British birth.

"I suppose you've learnt French as well as Arabic," I said.

"No, that is hardly any use in the Legion; 90% of them are German, so I've learnt a lot of that. Only the commands are given in French."

"But what would happen if the war starts?"

"The French know they could never use the Legion against the Germans. Although they are nearly all in it because they have run away from the Nazis, they would never fight them. Some are even proud of them."

"What do you mostly do here?" I asked.

"We go up and down the country keeping peace between the Arabs and the Jews."

As we drove back to the town, still talking, he said, "Would you like to come and see the barracks?"

"Yes, please," I answered, my mind filled with pictures of austere forts placed in the middle of a burning desert, no shade for miles. We drove on through the town and there, sure enough, in the middle of the burning desert was a large mud fort — low, square and faintly menacing. One side was pierced by a large gate which was closed and barred. Beside it was a small postern. Michael opened it and ushered me in. There before us spread a big, sunny square, with flowering oleander bushes, and seated at small tables under brightly coloured umbrellas were the Legionnaires, sipping long, cool drinks.

Next morning Elsie was much better and as keen as I to push on. I think that the long rest in bed was really what she needed. We neither of us perhaps realised quite what a shock it must have been to her system to do this journey, especially coming to this heat from the English climate. I had hardly been doing anything else but travel for the last three years, so was thinking of this as a luxury trip. For her, at her age, it must have been very hard at times, but she never complained and was always cheerful. In the end we compromised and she stayed in bed all morning and then we left late in the afternoon and only drove for about four hours before camping out for the night.

So the days went by, driving, sightseeing and bathing in the Mediterranean. One day, as we were snoozing under our canvas shelter and getting no relief from the brisk, hot wind that was blowing, a bicycle came past with a mast attached to the seat and a sail boomed out. A solid, fair-haired man was pedalling and, in a flash, before we could stop him, he was gone. I thought that on the long, empty road we would be sure to overtake him and be able to find out how far he had travelled on such a practical vehicle, but we never saw him again.

When we came to Tripolitania, Mussolini's show-place, we could not help but contrast it quite favourably with Algeria. The beautifully tarred road stretched for hundreds of miles without a break to the Egyptian border; the Roman ruins were all cared for and partly restored. I had the best bathe of my life, diving into the clear blue Mediterranean off a marble balustrade. But the modern Italian effort to compete with the Romans was rather pathetic; an enormous marble gateway planted across the road in the middle of the empty desert, looking to us exactly like Marble Arch. As the Baby Austin hummed along the tarmac, it would be a crowded day if we saw six vehicles. Italian road-gangs were stationed every 50 miles, and they lived in fear in their little fortresses. In Tobruk, on the outskirts of the town, we saw a large, barbed-wire cage where some starving Arabs were dragging out their lives. The Italians claimed that they were not imprisoned but were only there to save them from attack by other Arabs. Whatever the reason, they were quite clearly dying of sickness, hunger and despair.

The little car did amazingly well; twice during our midday stops I put on my bathing cap and crawled underneath to give it a greasing. It arrived in good shape at the Egyptian frontier, a break in the barbed-wire that stretched from the sea over 100 miles inland, marking the border between the two countries in the featureless desert.

For us it was only too plain that we had left Mussolini's domain because we had also left the road. Down the escarpment there was a fairly well-defined track, but when we got to the bottom there were only a few wheel-marks in the sand, branching out in all directions. It was quick decisions all the time, because if the wheels stopped for even a second, we were stuck, which meant having to unload everything while we pushed her out and ran her on till we got on to a firm piece of ground. Then we were faced with the portage of all the gear.

After we had left Mersa Matruh and were on a rough but recognisable road, I got careless. We were travelling along, planning what we would do when we reached Alexandria, when I saw, too late, a large ditch across the road into which we dropped. With appalling exertions we managed to get out again and saw that the whole chassis seemed to have collapsed sideways. However, as the engine was still going and the wheels turned, though with difficulty, we limped along till we came to a railway line with a small station. The Egyptian in charge was charming and mercifully spoke French. He told us that there was a miller who lived only two miles away and that this miller was a talented man who would fix our car in no time. So we limped on to the miller's house. He was a Copt and an even better man than we had been told. He invited us to stay the night and mended the springs which had broken. He made them out of scrap iron and charged me practically nothing.

It was just a day's drive from the miller's on to Alexandria, and there Elsie left me to stay with her sister, also a Moslem, who was waiting to go on a pilgrimage to Mecca and was then in the process of spending the necessary three years in a Moslem country, a rule that is strictly enforced for every convert to the Moslem religion wishing to make the pilgrimage.

I went to Port Said via Cairo and then got on the boat for Bombay where I was expecting Miles to meet me. In Bombay there was only a telegram saying that he could not meet me as he was playing in a polo tournament but that he had got a house. Being married had made a difference already.

When the Baby Austin was offloaded on the quay, and I put my two suitcases in it, I looked again at the telegram and wondered for the first time about our house. I knew that we could hire furniture, but it would need something more than hired furniture to make it look like a home. The last time I had lived in India I had had with me all English things — linen, crockery, cutlery, pictures and other household treasures. Now I was starting a new life and, to make the change complete, I thought it would be fun to have everything we needed made in India by Indians.

I started in Bombay with the house linen, most of which I bought from the big Indian cotton mills, but for the table linen I went to the Congress shops, started by Gandhi and run by the Congress Party, where they sold only hand-woven, hand-spun, Indian cottons that were dyed with local vegetable dyes. This added some extra weight to the car when I set off to do the 600-odd miles to Gwalior, where I planned to buy the crockery. The rainy season was on, the dirt roads muddy, and most of the rivers were in flood and had to be crossed on makeshift ferries, so I was glad enough to have to spend two nights at the rest house in Gwalior. The manager of the pottery works did everything to help. He showed me over the entire workshop. He let me choose exactly what I wanted; my own colour scheme, the design for the colours, and also the shapes of the plates and cups and dishes. The only snag was that I would have to wait six weeks for delivery.

Another 600 miles got me up to Lahore, where Miles met me so we could go together to Baluchistan where his regiment was stationed. On the way we stopped in Multan for our last bit of household shopping. For hundreds of years Multan has been famous for its silk weavers. We drove through the old Indian city down the narrow streets to where the weavers worked, and from the man whose family would do the actual weaving we ordered our curtains and loose covers.

We really only camped in our house, as we knew that in nine months, when Miles' "long leave" came round, we would be going away again. We were full of plans; first we were going to climb the Himalayas, after which we would go east and west respectively, to visit relations, and then meet again in British Columbia where we wanted to look for some land we could farm when we retired. Our climbing trip was cut short when Miles read a Stephen King-Hall newsletter prophesying war by the end of August or the first week in September.

So we came down from the snow and, in the heat of the plains, plunged into preparations for our separate journeys. Since war was so obviously on its way, I clung to my Boxer passport. I had my letter of credit, too, made out in that name. Sometimes it seems as if army regulations are made to suit the wilder married men. At the first hint of trouble, all kinds of restrictions, if not actual banishment, descend on the hapless "dependants", as the wives and children are called, and the vacuum they leave behind is very often partly filled by other single women with all kinds of odd qualifications. I thought that as Miss Boxer I might join their ranks.

We parted at Lahore station, Miles to go west to see his mother, and me east. It was an exciting parting with the future so uncertain. We had no real idea where we would meet again, though we hoped it would be in Canada.

CHAPTER TEN
INTO BURMA

I STARTED my journey right away by travelling third class, which was like arriving in a new country. Travelling first or second class I would have been just one of a herd of "Memsahibs". My dealings with the Indians would be influenced by preconceived notions of what Memsahibs thought or needed. Memsahibs never travelled third but if they did, the Indians would regard them as special if not extraordinary individuals. There was also the extra attraction of third class being unbelievably cheap. The 1,300 miles from Lahore to Calcutta cost, in those days (1939), about 25 shillings.

It was uncomfortable and very dirty, but there was also an air of gaiety and a strong smell of food as each group — Indian women never travelled singly — arrived, carrying a pile of provisions. These Indians, according to Indian standards, were not badly off. The really poor could not afford the fare and would always walk, no matter how great the distance, as time was a thing they did not worry about.

We all made our own little burrows, and I chose the top shelf. I did not know if it was actually intended for passengers or only for luggage, but it was by far the best place, as it was quite out of reach of the children. The lavatory conditions were appalling; not entirely due to the women themselves, but more to bad design. It must have been designed in England by a man who had vaguely heard of India and had been told that the inhabitants had rather different methods of sanitation, which led him to believe that they

103

were also structurally different. I cheated in order to avoid using the lavatory. During the long waits at the main stations, I went to the first-class Ladies' Waiting Room. No one would have queried the ticket status of a European seen entering one.

In Calcutta I stayed with friends and tried to find out how I could get through to Burma overland, but my determination was not proof against all the advice I received and the difficulties I was told about. In the end I took a boat to Rangoon.

I had read a book called *Siamese White* about an 18th-century trader who had crossed to Bangkok from a coastal town in Lower Burma called Mergui. I was all set to do this too. In Rangoon I went to see one of the merchants who, I had been told, had some interests in the forest near Mergui. He regarded me with absolute horror.

"My dear young lady, you cannot possibly go that way," he said. "Now is the season of the rains and even our elephants cannot use the tracks."

Not quite sure how to take this comparison between me and his elephants, I turned to my second alternative. To go up by train to Taungyi, on the edge of the Shan States, and from there overland to the railhead in Siam and on down to Bangkok. It was a case of "the longest way round is the shortest way there". I would be going at least 400 miles north out of my way, but after I so cravenly failed to go overland from India, nothing was going to stop me going overland from Burma.

The monsoon I brushed off with a light-hearted remark that I had been in the monsoon in India and that I could easily manage. I went to the bazaar and bought myself a large black cotton umbrella, which cost me two shillings. I knew that no matter what advice I got in Taungyi, the only alternative to forwards would be backwards, and that I knew I could never face.

The third class on the Burma railways was an amazing contrast to India. I went in the "Ladies'" carriage, and it was only sparsely filled with delightful little ladies in beautiful silk *lungyis* hugged tightly round their narrow hips and tucked in at their tiny waists. Above a lovely smooth golden midriff they wore a short-sleeved silk blouse that was in turn covered by a starched frilled white organdie overblouse. Golden pins were in their shiny black hair, and the only blot on their fairy-like appearance was the enormous cigars they constantly smoked, their mouths stretched wide to encompass them. They had a few equally immaculate children with them. The carriage was spotlessly clean, and so was the lavatory.

One young beauty was a trained medical nurse. She was travelling up to Meiktila and spoke good English. She took me under her wing, ordering my food from vendors on the platform. This was gracious travelling. The train passed through the valley of the Irrawaddy, an orderly country patterned with rice fields. They glittered green as the sun shone out after the rain.

A fresh smell of clean earth blew in through the open carriage windows and mingled with the fumes of the cigars. The rest of the Burmese ladies thawed quickly as the journey progressed. At least two of them had been to college and spoke good English. We talked and laughed a great deal and showed each other our clothes, mine looking singularly unattractive and clumsy in comparison with theirs. At one station we were invaded by a group of Indian women and children, and in five minutes the carriage was a mess. The Burmese clustered together at one side, with well justified looks of disgust on their faces, while the Indians spread their food around, throwing their orange and banana peels on the floor and spitting out the pips and other pieces of inedible food. The children urinated unconcernedly where they willed. I was amazed to think that I had ever travelled in such dirt and squalor and had taken it for granted. After two hours the Indians got out. At once the Burmese called the guard and asked for the carriage to be cleaned and, to my surprise, a sweeper came at once, swept it clean and sprinkled the floor with water.

Although I really liked Indians, I did not hesitate now to join in the general condemnation, always keen to be on the right side of present company. Now all the women became very friendly, and I realised that their position in society was certainly as good as ours. These women talked of the businesses that they were running, how they managed their family affairs, and what were their plans for the future. It was a little difficult to guess the husbands' part in their lives, as all but the nurse were married.

The husbands spent quite a lot of their time being monks and also, although it was not actually mentioned, did a certain amount of banditry in the outlying districts. While they were monks it must have been a nice change from their life with their intelligent managing wives. To have the mild little nuns to wait on their every need may even have been the principal reason for their religious devotion. A woman's position, from a religious aspect, was distinctly low.

Most of the women left the train at Meiktila and during the night I was alone. I asked the Burman guard to wake me up at the station before Taungyi so that I could tidy up.

"Where are you going to stay?" he asked.

"I don't know," I said. "Could you recommend me a good Burman hotel?"

"Oh, you must go to Miss Watson, she takes in single ladies, you will be comfortable there." Then he added, with a disparaging glance at my clothes, "She is not expensive."

It was still dark when he woke me up, and not long after I was ready, having taken great pains over my appearance in order to try to keep up to Burman standards, the train came to a halt. The guard arrived and quickly arranged with a coolie to take my bag and show me the way to Miss Watson.

We had climbed up since leaving Meiktila to over 4,000 feet, and dawn came up from the hills, rosy and glistening. There had been heavy rain and the path, bordered with lovely trees, was about two inches deep in slippery mud. It was cool and fresh, birds sang, and the gentlest morning breeze brought to me the sweet scent of jasmine. I had a feeling that things would go all right for me here.

Taungyi was on a shelf above the Yaungwhe plain, and behind and round it were the first row of hills that separated Taungyi from Kentung, where I was planning to go. Here was no dirty town with streets filled with poverty-stricken hungry people that I had learnt to expect in the east. This was an enlarged village, with some poor, of course, but none hungry.

Miss Watson lived in a European-style bungalow. A small gate opened onto a garden, and the path leading to the house between flower-beds was tarred. Except for the exotic flowers, I might have been in Wimbledon. Miss Watson, round and friendly, with grey curly hair just pinned up any old way to keep it from bothering her, opened the door. She smiled a welcome but looked surprised to see me.

"Did you send a telegram?" she asked. "I had not heard that anyone was coming, and the road has been closed by rain."

"I am looking for a place to stay for a few days," I said. "The guard on the train told me that you sometimes took in visitors, and I was hoping that you would have room for me."

She smiled. Her faded blue eyes had that childlike, trusting look so many dedicated missionaries have, which, when confronted by human failings, turns to a look of hurt bewilderment.

"Well, it is just missionary ladies who stay with me," she answered, "but I have nobody here now and could easily put you up. There is indeed nowhere else except the rest house, and it would be difficult there without a servant. What is your name?"

"Beryl Boxer," I answered promptly. I would have to cash some of my traveller's cheques here and thought that it would save involved explanations if I stuck to the one name. In a small place like this, discussing a stranger was always a welcome change from the normal conversational diet.

As I followed her into the house, my mind was churning busily over her remark about the road being closed for the monsoon. The road she referred to was almost certainly the one to Kentung, which was where I wanted to go, and was the only one acknowledged as a road by the P.W.D. P.W.D. was the abbreviation for Public Works Department, and throughout India and Burma it was in charge of all roads and Government buildings. As most white people lived in Government-owned houses, the poor P.W.D. were usually unpopular. I had heard that the road was mainly a riding or walking track but it was wide enough and good enough to take a small car in the good season. If Jeeps or Landrovers had existed then, it would have been easy for them.

The house was exactly like many of the houses I had been in in England, visiting friends of my mother's who had retired after years in the East. There were the same chintz covers and silver-framed photographs placed among assorted brass and ivory gods and carvings. Only when breakfast was carried in by a young Karen girl was I reminded that I was actually in Burma.

Miss Watson was one of those really good people who could only have a beneficial effect on anyone who knew her, and as I came to meet the rest of the missionaries, they too turned out to be the kindest I had ever met. They were all Baptists, and the Karens were all Baptists too, which may have accounted for the general air of happiness that pervaded the little town.

Nobody seems quite sure who the Karens originally were or how many of the smaller tribes calling themselves by other names are also of Karen stock, but for the passing visitor like me they were all Karens. They are mainly agriculturalists, simpler and less sophisticated than the Burmese. Whether they were an offshoot from the Burmese or had come in from China, they had brought with them a legend, passed down through centuries, that white men with hair on their faces and carrying a book would come from the West and tell them about the true God. When the first missionaries arrived in Victorian times, coming from the West with their beards and white faces, the Karens could not get baptised fast enough. As the word spread that the white men with beards had arrived, so the villagers came in from the outlying valleys. It happened that the first missionaries were Baptists, so now practically all the Karens are Baptists. Later came other missionaries, but they made hardly a dent in the solid wall of Baptists. There were still Buddhists, and Buddhists are so tolerant that it never bothered them if their followers took out extra insurance with another religion.

It was good that the Buddhists also throve, because their religion added more than any other to the beauty of the country and town. Almost every one of the hills circling the town had its quota of white pagodas and *stupas*, looking, when they had been freshly whitewashed, as if they were made out of icing sugar. The little bells hanging round their eaves gave a happy, tinkling sound.

Miss Watson was a teacher, but as the holidays were on, she had free time, and after I had had a bath I asked her about my chances of getting on to Kentung. She was quite optimistic.

"The road is called 'closed', and as far as we are concerned, it is. Our missionaries never travel on it during the monsoon and, so far as I know, neither do the natives, but there is a Chinese who runs the Dak and goes once a month. He will be leaving in, I think, three days."

"Oh, that would suit me perfectly. I had better go straight off to the post office and see what I can fix up."

"It's not far," said Miss Watson. "I will come with you and then I will do my shopping and we can come back together."

We walked along the lovely, tree-shaded road and came to the place where all the Government buildings were gathered, including the post office, surrounded by shady trees. With its steps and wide verandah it looked more like a private house than a post office. I crossed the verandah and went into the office proper where I asked to see the postmaster, who was a delightful Burman, charmed to stop his work and talk to me.

"Of course I will ask Ah Fong if he will take you with him, but," he added in troubled tones, "I don't know if he will. He is a funny fellow and does not seem to like people. But he is the only man who will run the mail in the monsoon, and I cannot make him take you if he does not want to."

"Well, it is only that I need someone to carry my stuff and to show me the way. I can look after myself and will bring or buy my own food," I pleaded. He shook his head, looking as sad as his cheerful face could.

"Please do not be too sure. I will do my best, but Ah Fong is very difficult. I will speak to him this evening. Come back tomorrow and I will tell you what he says."

I bowed myself out with many thanks and went back on the verandah. There Miss Watson was already waiting. She was anxious to show me all that the mission was doing, but as we walked to see the school, the chapel and the recreational hall, my eyes were more on the passers-by, in their colourful dresses, each carrying an oiled paper or a silk umbrella. These were a splendid protection against the rain, and if used as a sunshade, they cast a becoming shade on the face. There were also monks in their orange robes, carrying their black wooden begging bowls, looking so well-fed that they were walking testimonies to the generosity of the local inhabitants.

Taungyi will always remain in my mind as a kind of Jane Austen place. Miss Watson and I spent our entire day walking about and paying little visits, doing good works in a gentle, easy fashion, and attending tea parties. In between I would go and visit the post-master and sip green tea with him while he told me how the bargaining with Ah Fong was getting along. Gradually, as the negotiations proceeded, I began to get a clearer picture of where I was going. The Dak, or post, went as far as Kentung and, even in the dry season, did not go beyond to the Siamese border.

I could not find out anything about the conditions beyond Kentung. Not that I tried very hard, as my first objective was to get to Kentung and that was difficult enough. It was obvious that Ah Fong did not want to take me. I had, of course, been gradually increasing the price I was prepared to pay. Finally we agreed on the use of his mules for my baggage and his company for the distance of about 250 miles — a journey of about ten days if we were not too delayed by swollen rivers.

The postmaster was distressed because Ah Fong did not do the regular stages of about 15 miles at a time, where there would be a Government rest house where I could have stayed. He intended doing it in longer stages. He had his own camping sites where there was grazing for his mules.

We had a little celebration, an after-dinner coffee party at Miss Watson's, the night before I left. I was given several things to take to the Kirkmans, who were the Baptist missionaries in Kentung. There was medicine and other things that they did not want to trust to the post, so I was put in charge. I was quite sorry to be going; it was such a happy, harmless place, and with the threat of war always on my mind, I found that I was looking at everything with new eyes.

I did not have much stuff to pack, having sent my tidy clothes by post from Rangoon, and by the far the most important piece of equipment was my large black umbrella. Although not as attractive as the Burmese ones, it was far more durable, and I had been using it constantly in Taungyi. Having been warned of the danger from malaria, particularly now the rains were on, I had designed and made a travelling mosquito net. I already had a silk sleeping bag. I found it better than a cotton one, as it was not as miserable to lie in when soaking wet. This was before the era of plastics. Treated canvas or rubber were the only waterproof materials, but they were very heavy and the rubber did not take long to turn sticky in the tropics.

My mosquito net was made in the form of a large bag, big enough so that I could open the umbrella inside it. I would get into my sleeping bag and put the umbrella into the net bag, open it and hold it well above my shoulders. With my free hand I made sure that the sleeping bag came inside the lower end of the net, then I lay down. The sleeping bag covered me to the shoulder, the net bag came down to my waist, and the opened umbrella kept the net from touching my face and arms as I lay. By running a tape through the bottom hem of the mosquito net bag, I could tighten it round my waist so that it could not work up and at the same time it held the silk bag up. It would, I hoped, be completely mosquito-proof. It took up hardly any room and was light as a feather.

So far, living in a house in Taungyi, the rains had not seemed too bad, but now I was going to be all day and night out of doors. One problem that I never solved was my shoes, which were deplorable. The only ones that I found comfortable were the Chinese cotton-soled shoes, but in the wet they got limp and difficult to keep on. My ankles are weak so I had to take crepe bandages for them. I had to wear trousers as protection from leech bites. To carry my personal things I bought a Shan bag. All the Karens use them, both men and women, and the missionaries too.

These bags were simply made and all the same shape and size. The price depended on the material. They were all hand-woven from cotton, the cheapest being made of coarse unbleached cloth, while the most expensive had silver and gold threads woven in, and sometimes additional decorations of seeds or beads. I bought a medium-priced one of gay colours and later wished that I had had the sense to buy two or three.

It rained heavily in the night and was still raining when I said goodbye to Miss Watson early in the morning. With a coolie carrying my baggage, I slipped and splashed my way to the post office to join the Dak. The first sight of Ah Fong outside the post office was not encouraging. He was small and singularly dismal-looking for a Chinese. With him, besides the Dak mules, was a small boy of about 13. As the postmaster introduced us, Ah Fong tried to smile, but I could see he was not accustomed to it. The little boy was bursting with excitement and importance. It must, I think, have been his first trip.

Ah Fong took my pack and the small sack of emergency tins, and put them in a pannier on one side of a mule. The Dak was very small and light, a load for one mule, but there were four altogether, one saddled for riding. As he covered up the pannier with a leather cover against the rain, he talked earnestly to the postmaster who listened, then, turning to me, said, "Ah Fong is a hard man. He says to tell you that you must look after yourself. You must not ask the boy to help you as he has enough to do looking after the mules."

"Yes, that's alright, please tell him that I understand."

I tried to look as gloomy and severe as Ah Fong himself, thinking that perhaps he would prefer me to look as dismal as he did. This was not hard to do because the rain was still drenching down. I opened my umbrella and waited. Ah Fong cast an expert eye over the mules' gear, said a few words to the boy and, with a wave of his hand and a low command, jumped on his mule and moved off.

I said goodbye to the postmaster and thanked him. At the last minute he looked a bit upset, asking me if I was sure that I wanted to go. I fell into line behind the boy, who walked after the mules, Ah Fong riding ahead of the procession. My umbrella was perfect protection; there was no wind and the rain fell vertically, so I was dry and much cooler than in a raincoat.

Ah Fong led off at a brisk pace and kept on for hours without a halt, but the weather helped me as the rain stopped and the sun came out. The birds too came out from the sheltering trees. The mynahs chattered as they searched for food, but the hoopoes were much the most attractive with their lovely colouring and elegant crest. At first we went through cultivated land, where the terracing looked so neat after the untidy fields of India. The road was firm and well-graded so I could walk looking about me instead of at where to put my feet.

When we came to the forest, it too was tidy, and sometimes I could see orchids high up in the branches. The boy ran along behind the mules, occasionally casting a smile towards me, but, intimidated by Ah Fong's stiff back, we did not try to talk. As the hours went by, it was all I could do to keep up, and I was thankful when, having lost sight of the mules for about five minutes, I rounded a bend to find them all clustered together at the side of the road being unsaddled. Ah Fong had started a little fire going, but I moved across to the other side of the road, determined to prove myself independent. We had a good rest of an hour or more and, by the time the mules were saddled again, I felt I could carry on. The rest of the day passed in a haze of fatigue. We stopped for the night by a small grassy patch, with grazing for the mules and a small leaf shelter, just a roof of leaves on four legs. This I shared with Ah Fong and the boy, but I was too tired to cook, contenting myself with opening a tin and gobbling its contents. My mosquito net worked very well.

I was stiff and tired in the morning when I heard Ah Fong and the boy start their fire, but after a cup of hot cocoa made on my own fire, I felt ready for anything. We moved off directly it was light, travelling in alternate rain and sun, and mostly in silence till our noonday stop. By this time I had decided that I would eat my main meal at midday, as I was less tired then and there was no danger of being overtaken by darkness while I was still organising myself.

In the afternoon we passed through a small village and I managed to buy some eggs, but two of them turned out to be bad. At the far end of the village there was a little river, where I stopped to bathe my feet and watch with envy the girls and women bathing. The Burmans and Karens are all fanatically clean and had two or three baths daily. Standing on the bank, they would slip off their blouses and pull up their *lungyis* to cover their breasts. Then they would walk down into the water and gracefully submerge to do their washing. Once they were under water nothing could be seen, as the water, particularly in the rains, was a rich tea colour.

On the third day my stiffness had gone and I felt fine. During the day we crossed several small streams, now risen to twice their normal height and over waist-deep. I would wait till Ah Fong and the boy were out of sight and then wade across without my trousers. Away from the villages we never met anyone. In the evening we came to a broad river. Even in the dry season it would have to be crossed by a ferry, but now, in the monsoon, it was a red-brown torrent, flowing fast. Since during the morning the ferry had been damaged in a sudden spate, Ah Fong would have to wait till the ferry was mended. It was already late afternoon, so that meant spending the night.

There was a P.W.D. gang there and also, to my joy, a Dak bungalow. These bungalows were a feature of India and Burma and were built by the Government, before the days of mechanical transport, for officials on tour, when they depended on ponies and bullock carts. They were furnished with tables and chairs and *charpoys*, the Indian version of a bed which had webbing woven between the four legs instead of springs; this also acted as a mattress and was delightfully cool. There was a caretaker, who would sometimes keep hens and sell a few eggs or even the birds themselves.

Leaving Ah Fong in his austere little camp, I went up to the bungalow. I could see that there was a fire in the cook-house, which meant that it was occupied, and when I reached the bungalow itself, I found the P.W.D. officer for the district there. He was a tall, good-looking Moslem from the Punjab and spoke excellent English. He gave me a great welcome and a wonderful tea with quantities of sweet biscuits.

"What a pleasure it is for me to meet a lady here. My name is Ata Mohammed. You are wanting to cross the river, I suppose, but first you will have to spend the night here. Please be my guest."

After only two nights on the road, I was absolutely thrilled with the hospitality. Mohammed called his servant and told him to get me a hot bath, and in no time I was soaking in a small tin tub, waist-deep in hot water. My legs folded in the Buddha position gave me an unattractive close-up of my very dirty feet. A little later, my legs stretched out on a long chair and a drink in my hand, I thought with no envy at all of Ah Fong and the boy camping so uncomfortably in the open.

"How is Rangoon?" Ata Mohammed asked me anxiously, as soon as he had seen to my comfort.

"Well, it seemed alright. I did not stay long, but the monsoon is a good one."

"No, no, I don't mean that, but is it safe? Are there riots?" Then I realised. In 1937 Burma had got independence from India and one of the first things that happened was that most of the Indians in Government Service were eased out of their jobs on one pretext or another and replaced by Burmans. Many Indians remained, particularly on the various plantations. Their lower standard of living made them much disliked and eventually this feeling had broken out in severe riots during which several hundreds of Indians had been killed.

Ata Mohammed was worried. "My father came over with the British in the early days. I have been born here, and so have my sons. Now what are we to do? My family has done well in Burma but for my sons it will be impossible. I have a nephew also in the P.W.D. who has become a Burman, but for him it is easier as his mother is Burmese." He shook his head and sighed.

It was indeed difficult for him. The main dislike the Burmans had was for the Indian labourers, who had come over in such numbers from India to work on the rubber plantations. The Burmans themselves, having such a rich country with a large export surplus of rice, saw no reason to work. They had no population problem and seemed to be able to control their birth rate; at least they did not appear to have the enormous families that are to be seen all over India. The labouring Indians were Hindus from the south and altogether different from Ata Mohammed. His colouring was not darker than that of the Burmans themselves, while the coolies were as dark as negroes; but he could never hope to pass himself off as a Burman, since his size alone would betray him, that and his noble nose and deep-set eyes.

It was difficult to know what to say. I felt deeply in sympathy with the Burman point of view, brought home to me so clearly by the Indian invasion of the "Ladies'" carriage. Yet here, as Ata Mohammed's guest, I could well imagine how he felt if he and his family were to have to return to India with its appalling population problem; there they could not hope to keep the high standard of living they had got accustomed to in Burma.

In my turn I tried to find out if he had heard any international news. He was very surprised that I should be worrying over news from Europe. We cheered each other up as we gloomed our way through an excellent curry and rice.

"I have bought some property in Burma. It was for my old age; now what can I do? The Burmans will come one day and kill us all."

"My husband is a soldier and has gone back to England. If Germany goes to war, he will fight and may easily be killed like my father was in the last war," I answered, in an endeavour to take his mind off his own problems. At that time it was surprising to meet people in the East whose whole life was being uprooted because of politics. In the East politics were still in their infancy after many years of settled rule.

CHAPTER ELEVEN
"SHE IS RATHER LIKE ME"

E ARLY next morning I rejoined Ah Fong, feeling very rested after my comfortable night. We crossed the river on a temporary ferry made of two native boats tied side-by-side with planks lashed across them for the mules to stand on. Ah Fong got them on with no trouble, but then he was a very forceful character. All day we walked on at a rapid pace through alternate patches of cultivation and forest through almost continuous rain and occasional sunshine.

We came just after our midday halt to a large village. I saw that it had a tea-shop — not a very smart one — consisting of a roof of leaves supported by four poles. Large puddles lay on the floor, showing how it leaked in the rain. Some planks laid across sections of tree-trunks served as seats. Ah Fong had disappeared into one of the houses, leaving the boy to look after the mules, so I seized the opportunity to have a rest and a cup of tea.

As soon as I was seated, the crowd began to gather. The women pressed close round me, touching my hair and face and fingering my clothes, all the time smiling their stained-tooth smiles. They stood round me in their neat pretty *lungyis*, their long shining hair pinned with gold or silver pins. Some of the older women were still wearing the old-style Paungthu dress, all black with a black turban and hammered-silver ornaments, but, old and young alike, these dainty, doll-like creatures had red lips and blackened teeth; sometimes a full set, sometimes with gaps, but all a dark reddish-brown, shading in some cases to pitch black. This was the result of

116

chewing betel nut. In India people chewed betel nut, and I had done it myself. It had a nice astringent taste and was a wonderful settler after an enormous Indian meal. But I had never seen Indians with teeth discoloured like these.

I ordered tea, and when it came the women moved aside and squatted down in a circle about me, watching my every move, smiling and talking quietly among themselves. As soon as they saw that I had finished, they clustered round again and this time they noticed the fob-watch I was wearing. It was like a little glass ball with a watch inside, and the works, ticking away busily, absolutely fascinated them. To the watch-face they paid no attention at all.

Suddenly the crowd round me was rudely thrust apart and Ah Fong appeared, beckoning imperiously. I paid up quickly and followed him. The whole crowd accompanied us to the outskirts of the village, and among them I saw a tall young Sikh of about 22 or 23. When all the villagers had said goodbye, he still remained, and when he came up beside me and started to talk, it dawned on me that he too was travelling to Kentung. I knew no Burmese, and he had only very little English, but with my smattering of Urdu and his Punjabi we could understand each other well enough. I did not take to him. Although tall and well-built, he had a very sly air about him, and he suffered from self-consciousness or inferiority or something like that, alternately boasting how much better he was than the Burmans and how he was completely unafraid of them, then telling tales of great atrocities they had committed and how careful Indians had to be.

By evening I was thoroughly fed up with him. As soon as we stopped for the night and Ah Fong and I started to light our fires, he rushed off into the bush and came back with an armful of wood that I did not need.

"Memsahib, Memsahib, look what good wood I have found for you!" he exclaimed, as he laid it at my feet. He then bustled round the fire getting hopelessly in my way. I grabbed up some of my wood and pressed it on him.

"Now you must make your own fire; I wish to eat my meal," I said.

Giving me a hurt look he answered, "I understand, Memsahib, it is because I am Indian that you do not wish me near you," and he moved off into the darkness, every line expressing race-consciousness.

117

From their fireside Ah Fong and the boy regarded us sardonically. This part of my journey now turned into a sort of running engagement between Gulab Singh, as he was called, and me. If we came to a tea-house, he would wait till the crowd gathered round and just as we were all getting on famously, Gulab Singh would suddenly appear and start pushing them away, saying, I imagined, "Leave the Memsahib alone; white people do not like this behaviour." As the only word I understood was "Memsahib", I could only judge by results what he had actually said, but the people always left instantly, looking embarrassed and apologetic, and I could do nothing to bring them back.

When we started on again I would ask him, "What did you say to those people?"

"I just told them that the Memsahib did not like the smell of natives." Then he would give me a sly look. Trying to control my temper I would say, "That is absolutely wrong; you must promise never to say that again. I like the villagers and want to talk to them. You must leave me alone in the villages."

"Oh, Memsahib, very sorry, Memsahib; the Memsahib is such a good person, not like all other Memsahibs who do not like to have dirty natives crowding round them."

The next day the same thing happened again, and again I asked him why he had interfered. "Oh, Memsahib, so very sorry, but I thought that the Memsahib looked very tired, face getting all sweaty, so I told the people to give her a rest."

And so we battled on, but certainly he enjoyed it more than I, largely I suppose because he always got the better of me.

One day when we had not passed any villages, he came and stood beside me while I cooked my rice. He had not done it for a couple of days and I wondered why he was doing it now. As I began to eat, he watched each mouthful going down with a doleful expression on his face, like a hungry dog.

"What's the matter, Gulab Singh?" I asked. "Have you run out of food?"

"Yes, Memsahib," he answered sadly.

My conscience pricked me and I gave him half of mine, telling him that it was all I could spare as I did not know when I could get any more.

Next evening he was round again begging, so I asked him, "Why did you not get food in the village?"

"No money left, Memsahib."

"What will you do in Kentung if you have no money left?"

"That is easy, Memsahib; in Kentung is my father's brother; he will be glad to see his brother's child; he will look after me."

"But if he cannot give you money, what will you do then?"

"Oh, then I go on to Chieng Mai; there lives my mother's brother." I was appalled by this information and decided then and there that I would get out of Kentung as soon as possible for I could not conceive anyone really taking to Gulab Singh. In the meantime, here he was begging off me, so I shared out again, feeling very foolish as I saw the contemptuous look on Ah Fong's face; he would never have allowed such weakness.

"This is the last food I can give you. I am running out myself and I do not know when I will be able to buy any more," I said and hoped I sounded as if I meant it.

Next day we came to a tiny village. It had no little stall so I tried to buy some rice at one of the houses. Either the people could not understand or they did not want to sell, so I moved on. I was not too worried. If I did not give any more to Gulab Singh, I should have enough to last. The only trouble was that I did not have any idea how long we would be. We were doing about 25 miles a day, but it was mainly a question of where the villages were, as Ah Fong did not always follow the road. Also, there might be rivers so badly in flood that we would be held up.

Ah Fong had stopped the mules a little farther up the street and, looking back as I came up beside him, I saw the wretched Gulab Singh still outside the hut I had tried to buy rice from. I could see him waving his arms and hear him shouting. Then one word came clearly down the street. It was "Memsahib". I turned and hurried back.

"What are you trying to do?" I asked.

"I am telling these fools that they must sell the Memsahib rice when she wants it, otherwise she will tell the D.C. what bad people they are."

An old man now came out of the house with about a couple of pounds of rice on a plate which he offered to me. By now my pecker was up and I refused to buy it. I stood there and told Gulab Singh to go on ahead as I wanted to make certain that he would not take it. I was sure he would never pay for it. We left that village, and it turned out to be the last one where we could have

119

bought any food. I could tell by the milestones that we should only have a couple of days more, given a little luck, and I could do without food for a day if necessary. Gulab had quite settled down to sponging off me in the evenings. In exchange for my grudging handouts he collected the firewood.

That night I saw by the milestones that we only had about another 28 miles to do, so I rashly cooked all the food, thinking we would get in next evening. We shared it out sitting under my umbrella, as it was pouring with rain. It rained most of the night too, and next morning we were late in getting started. Then we could only creep along, as the road was so bad. We must have gone off on a detour and I had no idea, as we slid and struggled over some appalling steep slopes, what speed we were making. Suddenly, just as dusk was overtaking us, we stepped out on a wide graded track that could, and as I saw from some tire marks actually had, taken a car.

Ah Fong started to make camp. It had stopped raining and I tried to ask him how far Kentung was. He smiled, held up ten fingers, pointed to the setting sun, covered his eyes with his hands and shook his head. I took this to mean that Kentung was ten miles away and that it would be difficult to see in the dark so it would be better for me not to try. He was probably right and as we were stopped under a good shelter made by the road-workers, I thought I would do without dinner. I got my bedding arranged and sat down, made myself comfortable with my back against a large stone, got out an old magazine and tried to read it in the failing light. Gulab Singh came up smiling, with an armful of firewood which he laid at my feet. Hungry as I was, I could not help feeling intensely satisfied at being able to say, "No need to light the fire; there is nothing left to eat."

He looked at me quite unbelievingly. "But, Memsahib, I am hungry."

"So am I," I answered with great satisfaction.

Ah Fong and the boy had already got their fire going and their rice cooked and were looking across at us. Ah Fong said something to the boy, then, taking a fine porcelain bowl, filled it with rice and vegetables and sent it across to me. The boy put it in my hand, bowing as he did so. I bowed across to Ah Fong and thanked him and started to eat.

Gulab Singh waited, but when no more rice came across, finally he could bear it no longer and walked across to the other fire. I could not hear what he was saying but could easily guess. I had heard it too often myself in the last few days. Ah Fong was made of sterner stuff and he refused to part with as much as a grain of rice.

As I sat joyously lapping up the last of my food, I heard a curious humming noise that sounded vaguely familiar, and before I was able to identify what it was, I saw the reflections of head-lights, and round the corner crept a car. Its headlights swept across Ah Fong and his fire, then carried on till I was in its full glare. Then it stopped, the door opened and a tall figure got out. As he came into the light I saw it was an unusually tall Burman dressed in a *lungyi* and shirt. He came across to me holding out his hand.

"I am Maung Hsan, the P.W.D. officer; my bungalow is only three miles from here. I would be delighted if you would stay the night with me there; at least you will be more comfortable than here," he said. His eyes glanced over my bedraggled appearance. "I could also give you supper and a bath."

I was absolutely delighted with the idea. Ah Fong's gift of rice had only stimulated my appetite, and the idea of a bath, even if it was in a tin tub, was perfect.

"Could you please explain to Ah Fong?" I asked, "and tell him to take my things to the Kirkmans, and I will pay him there."

As I quickly rolled up my bedding and grabbed a few things that I would need for the night, I saw Gulab Singh approach Maung Hsan cringingly. It looked as if I was not alone in my dislike of Gulab because, with rather a curt answer, Maung Hsan then crossed over to me where I was finishing my packing and said, "Who is this man? Do you want him to come with us?"

"Good God, no!" I cried in horror.

I jumped into the car quickly, waving to Ah Fong and the boy, and as the headlights swept across their faces, for the first time I actually saw Ah Fong smiling with enjoyment as he contemplated the disconsolate figure of Gulab Singh.

We did not talk much as we drove the three miles through the darkness on the muddy road to the Dak bungalow. Then the car turned up a driveway and we saw the glow of oil lamps through the trees. We pulled up before a wide verandah with the usual two reclining chairs and the strip of coconut matting. A Burman servant came running out with a hurricane lamp in his hand. Maung Hsan took the lamp and held it up smiling.

"First I think we should wash our feet," he said.

I looked down at mine, and indeed he was quite right. I was covered in mud to half-way up my legs, and his were in no better state. He showed me into the little bathroom with its huge earthenware jug full of cool water, a large dipper laid across its mouth. An oblong galvanized bath was on the floor, and an old-fashioned wash-hand stand with basin and ewer. Beside the basin was a deep pot filled with water, and standing neck-deep in the water was an earthenware jug. This was a speciality of the Burmese Dak bungalows. The water in the outside bowl was drawn from a well or river, but by the time it had seeped through the porous sides of the earthenware jug, all impurities had been filtered away.

I had a good clean-up and heard welcome sounds of chopping and banging coming from the cook-house outside. When I got back to the verandah, Maung Hsan was already there looking very dashing in a clean, freshly ironed shirt and *lungyi*.

"Dinner will not be long now," he said. "What will you have to drink?"

I chose a fresh lime squash, and it was delicious when it came, cool from a porous jug hung up in the draft. As we sat in companionable silence sipping our drinks, I thought of the other Dak bungalow where I had met Ata Mohammed.

"Do you know Ata Mohammed who is also in the P.W.D.?" I asked.

"But of course; he is my uncle. Where did you meet him? Is he well?" he asked eagerly.

"At the first big river after Taungyi. The ferry was broken down and I spent the night at the bungalow."

Just then the Burman servant came in to say that dinner was ready, and we went indoors to the dining-room. We sat down at each end of an enormous, badly polished table, made, I imagine, out of teak, and the huge chairs were so heavy it was as well that the servant was there to push it close to the table for me. The light was from two guttering candles and, grouped round them at full arm's length from our chairs, was an astonishing collection of sauce bottles, most of the labels so spotted and torn that it was impossible to see what they were. The Burman servant suddenly materialized out of the dense blackness beyond the range of the candlelight, looking like a genie, bearing a great polished brass tray loaded with curry. This was Burmese curry, cooked with less fat than an Indian one and with little dried fish lurking among the vegetables.

I was longing to ask Maung Hsan how he was progressing with becoming a Burman. Sitting down like this at table so that you could not see how tall he was, his hair neatly covered by a gay little silk headcloth, I would never have thought he was an Indian. His English was spoken with the same accent as the postmaster of Taungyi, which was quite different from Ata Mohammed's.

After dinner, as we had coffee on the verandah, Maung Hsan himself started on the subject.

"I am so glad to hear news of my uncle," he said. "As a child, when my father was alive, I used to stay with him, and I loved him very much." He gave a sigh. "Now it is more difficult. Now I am a Burman, my mother is Burman, and I have to make the choice. After all, this is my country and the Burmans hate more than anything my father's people."

"Your uncle too is very worried about that. He does not know what to do, and it is even more difficult for his sons. If they go back to India they will find it hard to make such a good living there, and if they stay in Burma they risk their lives."

"What do you think I look like?" he asked after a short silence. "Did you think I was a Burman when you first saw me?"

"Yes, certainly. I just thought that you were unusually tall for a Burman, but I never guessed you were half Indian," I answered truthfully.

"Yes, perhaps I would fool a foreigner, but," and a look of fear crossed his face, "in a riot the Burmans would always know. If I could stay on here where I am known and where I am marrying a Burmese girl and the people know that I am a Buddhist, perhaps it will be all right, but I cannot see my Indian relations; I must treat them as if they were dead."

It was on this dismal note that I went to bed. This was all so familiar to me from my travels across Germany, where so many families with Jewish blood were going through the same problems. One thing all races, creeds and colours have in common is their way of persecuting each other, and it was to escape these gloomy thoughts that I fell asleep.

We were all up at daybreak, and after a good breakfast I started off to walk to Kentung. The Burman servant told me that Ah Fong had already passed on ahead. It was a lovely walk. I had had an excellent night and a good wash before starting; a welcome change after crouching in the damp and dismal dawn on a slippery mud bank above a coffee-coloured stream, wiping my face with water that left a thin film of reddish mud behind it; above all, the absolute bliss of being quite alone, though that was unfair to Ah Fong and the boy, who had never bothered me in any way. Although I knew Emerson's saying: "The power others have to annoy you, you give them," I did not get any help from it when faced with a man like Gulab Singh.

Kentung was above the river with high hills about it and everywhere were pagodas, some gleaming in their fresh coat of white paint and others crumbling away, because the Buddhists think it is better to build a new pagoda than repair an old one. I imagined that I could hear all their little bells ringing, but as I rounded a bend I found there was a *stupa* on the side of the road whose little bells I had heard. A monk came striding past me, the rain splashing off his black umbrella, his orange-coloured robe glowing against the background of dense green.

I came down into the town and passed through the crowded market-place and then on through the streets. The Kirkmans lived in the mission compound and I found it without any difficulty. They were expecting me, as Ah Fong was already there.

The mission was built round an open square formed by their house, the hospital and various outbuildings. Mrs. Kirkman, slight and pale, came out of the bungalow to meet me.

"How nice to meet you, Miss Boxer," she said. "It is such a joy to have a visitor in the monsoon. I cannot remember it happening before."

She came with me while I paid Ah Fong, who accepted the money with thanks. He did not attempt to ask for any extra, gave me one of his reluctant smiles and moved off with great dignity. I felt quite sorry to be seeing the last of him.

The inside of the bungalow was large, cool and dark, sparsely furnished with rattan furniture. It felt almost like home. All over the East, where the British have been, the P.W.D. put up almost identical houses. A central room with full-length doors and windows stretched through to the back verandah. Opening off each side of this room, depending on the size of the house, were two, three or four bedrooms and a dining- room. Off each of the bedrooms was a small square room with a tin bath and a toilet, nicknamed "thunder-box". I had lived for years in these sorts of houses; they had, of course, their little variations, but in the main the plan was always the same, which made it easy for any guests to find their way about.

As I unpacked the various parcels that I had brought with me, Mrs. Kirkman chattered away like people do when they have not seen any strangers for some time. It was Miss Boxer this and Miss Boxer that, which made me feel very awkward.

"Please call me Beryl," I said at last.

"And my name is Mary," she said. "We do hope that you will stay with us as long as you can, but I am sure Mrs. Butterworth will be asking you to go to them; she has heard that you have arrived and sent a note asking us all to drinks this evening. Her husband is commanding the detachment of the Burma Rifles stationed here."

Mary then looked straight at me. "I think," she went on, "when she finds you are not a missionary she will give you no peace unless you stay with her too."

"Well, I want to get on as quickly as possible and would like to start the day after tomorrow, if it would be possible to arrange it."

"Robin will be home to lunch quite soon and you must ask him. We always go back to Taungyi and I do not know much about the other way, but I think he will be able to fix something up for you."

At lunchtime Robin Kirkman came home from the hospital. He was small and quiet and seemed genuinely pleased to see me but could not disguise his distress at the idea of going out to drinks that evening.

"We are only two European families here," he explained, "and since the monsoon started we have not seen another white face. We all know each other so well and Mary and I don't drink, at least not wines and spirits."

"Well, dear," said Mary, "now Beryl is here we will have something new to talk about."

"What do you think my chances are of getting a coolie to go down to the railhead in Siam?" I asked, not entirely in order to change what was apparently a dangerous subject.

"You will be going through a bad malarial area," he said reflectively, "and although there is nothing that will immunize you, I will start you on some pills today that will prevent it breaking out for two weeks, and that should give you enough

125

time to get to the railhead. This afternoon I will make enquiries about getting coolies."

"I have hardly any stuff with me, and I am sure that one man could easily carry it," I said hastily. I was sure one coolie would be quite as much as I would be able to manage without speaking a word of his language.

That evening we all tidied ourselves up and left on foot for the party. The house was not very far, up on a hillside away from the town, with large trees in a big garden. It was already dark when we arrived and I could not see very well, but the scent from the flowers in the garden was delicious and, together with the golden glow of the oil- lamps, gave the place a slightly hedonistic air.

Major and Mrs. Butterworth came down the steps of the verandah as soon as we arrived. They were typically army, free and easy, fond of a bit of gaiety and a drink in the evening, not taking life too seriously, generous, kindhearted and not worried about other people's affairs.

Myra Butterworth seized me by the arm. "You must excuse me, Mary," she said, "but you have been able to find out all about her by now, and I am simply dying of curiosity."

She led me over to a table where the drinks were. A servant was already pouring out lemon squash for the Kirkmans.

"My dear," she hissed in my ear, "you don't look like a missionary; for heaven's sake say you will have a drink." She poured me out a generous portion of gin and took her time adding lime and water. I could see she did not want to say too much in front of the others.

"Can't you come and stay with us? Stay as long as you like; it would be such fun; you'll be driven mad by all the holiness down there."

Then, as I started to answer, she interrupted me, saying, "Don't you be embarrassed; I will tackle Mary myself," and over she went to Mary.

"Now, Mary, you must let Miss — oh, what is your name? — come and stay with us."

Mary, looking thoroughly distressed, started to answer, but I forestalled her; at all costs I did not want to get involved with a lot of entertainment.

"I am trying to get down to Chieng Mai, and Robin is making arrangements to get a coolie for me by the day after tomorrow."

"Oh, nonsense, I never heard of anything so ridiculous; you have only just arrived; you can't possibly dash off at once like that. You must come and stay, not another word about it. Now tell me where you have come from in India. Henry was seconded here from the Indian Army. I am sure you must know plenty of our friends."

I was feeling quite lightheaded myself by now, with my first drink for about three weeks and having got into this less rarefied air.

"I have been out visiting friends of mine. He is in Hodson's Horse. They are in Baluchistan; the Smeetons."

"Oh, marvellous, Henry knows the regiment very well, but did you say the Smeetons? We knew a Miles Smeeton, tall and good-looking, but he was not married."

"Yes, that is the same man; they only got married last year."

"Oh, not really? Do tell me what she is like."

I was rather taken aback by this question but, not liking to deviate too far from the truth, answered, "She is rather like me; we have been taken for sisters."

"Now you really must come and stay. Henry, what was the name of that couple in Hodson's? She had red hair and he was so gloomy."

The conversation rushed on, but by now the poor Kirkmans were quite out of it. Names were being bandied back and forth, and after my second drink I had to be on the alert to stop myself referring to Miles as my husband, and when Mary caught my eye in a pleading manner I was only too relieved to whisper to her that I was ready to leave.

At breakfast the next morning, Robin said that getting a coolie was being a bit of a problem. He had, however, got a convert called Loogale, who, though not a proper coolie, was keen to come, but first he had to get his wife's permission.

"Is that usual?" I asked. "Do they all have to get their wives' permission?"

"Yes, it's quite normal. Really the women run most of the business here and in a case like this, where carrying is not the husband's normal job, they would always consult their wives if not actually ask permission. Poor Loogale is a bit henpecked, I am afraid; perhaps that is one reason why he is so keen to get away."

This did not sound like the sort of coolie I would have chosen myself, but perhaps as he was already accustomed to being henpecked he would not mind being bossed around by me. Anyway, Robin was doing all the work for me so I could hardly fuss over his arrangements.

At lunchtime Robin came in with the splendid news that Loogale had said that his wife had given her permission for him to go with me on condition that I paid him half the money for the whole journey before we left so that he could hand it over to her.

"He never keeps a job very long, poor chap, so she wants to be sure that she gets her whack, but she won't let him go unless you pay, so you had better give him the money now," said Robin, laughing. Then he asked, "What have you got in the way of medicines?"

"Well, not very much; some Fructines Vichy for constipation and a bottle of something for dysentry, iodine, permanganate of potash, hydrogen peroxide, oil of cloves and a few bandages."

"Well, they are all quite safe. I will look through my stuff and see if I have anything that might be useful. About half-way, I think, there is a Catholic mission, and I have no doubt that if you were in difficulties they would help. I have never been on that road myself, so I do not know it, but sometimes patients from along it come up to the hospital. There is one village — I can't remember the name — but they are all lepers there; you should try to make sure not to spend the night in it."

This next part of the journey was, I thought, going to be much more interesting than the bit I had already done. There was no official road, so to speak, just the one the villagers used. I suppose the Government did not want to open up a good road to the various frontiers, as in that case they would have to install proper frontier officials with all the attendant expense. Travelling like this with one coolie and on foot, I would only be doing the walking stages of about 15 miles a day instead of the 25 I had done with Ah Fong. It also meant that I would be staying the nights in villages, which would mean a saving in carrying food, though Robin thought I should take at least 20 pounds of rice. As there were no Dak bungalows, the villagers themselves had worked out a system of catering for travellers. If they did not have a small hut put apart for them, the headman would allot the traveller to one family, each family taking its turn. It sounded the sort of thing that I most enjoyed and I was all on fire to start.

In the afternoon I went out to see Kentung and visit some of the temples. I liked the peaceful atmosphere they had, and they were always beautiful with the big, dark-red pillars and the beautifully dressed people sitting in little family groups or wandering around with their sticks of incense. I joined them, buying a couple of sticks and wandering round barefoot looking for the Buddha with the most sympathetic face in front of whom to light them. I sat down for a little while, watching the scented smoke rising in front of the images.

On my way back to the house I went to the bazaar and bought 25 pounds of rice and some salt to cook it with. When I got back to the house, Mary told me that Myra had sent a note to me.

"Do please come and stay," she wrote. "There are so many more of our friends we want to hear about. I am sure you could easily manage just a couple of days."

Now that I had Loogale fixed up and paid for, it was easy to write that I simply had to leave in the morning. The news from Europe was bad too. I felt that for that reason alone I should push on as fast as possible, so that when the war started I would be able to make arrangements by more normal methods of travel to get back to India. At that time no one considered the possibility of the Japanese coming in, and I was thinking of eventually getting back to Europe where Miles hoped to be and where I might be able to do something useful.

CHAPTER TWELVE
WITH AH KEE

I N the morning I was up before it was light and got my packing done. I decided to carry the rucksack myself more as a gesture than a necessity for there was hardly anything to put in it. It was one of those rucksacks with a carrying frame, and the Burmans hated it; they found the frame uncomfortable on their backs and it was awkward to carry any other way. Robin and Mary were always up at first light and so we had breakfast at the usual time and, to my surprise, Loogale turned up at the time he had said he would but carrying such a load for himself that by the time he took the rice, he could not manage much of mine. At the last moment a teenaged boy was pressed into service. He was surprisingly easy to get after all the trouble we had had in getting Loogale. It seemed a little odd that he had no female relative from whom to ask permission, and I wondered if perhaps it might not be some machination of Loogale's.

I said my goodbyes to Robin and Mary. Robin, looking rather unhappy, gave Loogale some last advice. Loogale seemed as reluctant to take it as Robin was to give it. With the boy carrying the rice and salt we started off. Our road led past the Butterworths' house, and I rushed by as I doubted if I had the strength of mind to refuse if they saw me and asked me in. I am always a bit nervous and excited at setting off on a trip like this, and it is only when I have really started and got right away on my own that I can relax and begin to enjoy myself. It is a hard thing to explain, and the question: "What difference can one day make?" is quite impossible to answer.

Above the Butterworths, isolated on a hilltop, was the last post office in Burma, and I called in to send a telegram to Miles to let him know that I was now on my last lap to Bangkok. The little Indian postmaster was delighted to have a visitor, and it was nearly an hour before I could get away, absolutely full to the brim with strong, sweet tea. All along this first part of the path there was the most wonderful terracing. I had not seen it so well done since I was in China.

I stepped along feeling very pleased with myself and wondering how the unfortunate uncle of Gulab Singh was getting on. Subconsciously I think he was the real reason for my immoderate haste to leave Kentung. It appeared to me impossible that the uncle would actually like him, in which case he would have to come on this, the only road to Siam where he had said, "My mother's cousin will be pleased to see me." I looked round behind me to see how the coolies were getting on. There was no sign of them, but it was lovely walking along by myself. The path led along the bank of a river and descended gently. It would be getting wetter and hotter as I went on and left the Shan Plateau and dropped down into Siam. Even now I thought that the forest I was passing through had thicker undergrowth and more hanging creepers.

Like the other road from Taungyi, there were not many travellers. I came to a large tree, clear of undergrowth and with a small platform in its lower branches with offerings of flowers and rice. A few bits of material hung from its lower branches. It was one of the "*Nat*" shrines. They were a survival from the time of spirit worship before Buddhism or Christianity. They were still used as a kind of extra insurance by the villagers. Any tree or rock that was a particularly fine specimen or had a freak shape might harbour one of these *Nats* or spirits, and they, although reputed to be malignant, were surprisingly easily placated by very small offerings of rice or flowers or pieces of cloth.

I found myself putting up my umbrella with increasing frequency and was glad at about two o'clock to come into a small village that had a little tea shelter. I sat down to wait for the coolies and ordered tea. The villagers began to gather round, the women coming close to finger my clothes while the men stood in a kind of outer circle feigning great indifference. They were a poor-looking lot, and their lives in the rainy season were sordid and uncomfortable. The whole village was covered in mud, and the houses, made as they were of split bamboo, did not do much towards keeping the rain out.

I rummaged in my rucksack and took out a book to read; also my exercise book in which I had written some local words. Robin had given me a list of words that I might find useful for dealing with Loogale and at overnight stops in villages; such words as: good, bad, please, thank you, how far? how much? too much, go on, stop, beautiful, slow and fast. I studied the list and tried to work out a sentence that I could greet Loogale with when he arrived. It was a full hour and a half before they appeared, soaking wet and complaining. They threw themselves in attitudes of greatest dejection down on the plank that served for a seat and were not at all cheered up when I ordered them tea.

"*Ma Ma,*" they cried, which I think meant something like mother or possibly aunt or sister. "Bad, bad."

I could see they were going to be a bit of a problem. I had my own problems, too, because this path had no nice milestones to tell me how far I had come, and I had no idea how the villages were spaced. I did not want to leave a village too late in the afternoon so that we would be unable to reach the next before nightfall. With foot coolies I could only do 15 miles a day, but in the mud and rain it was difficult to estimate distance, and Loogale himself did not know the way.

As I attempted to get them moving after their tea, they made much use of the words: "No good" and "Bad". This time I thought we had better keep together, so shepherded them carefully in front of me. At this the boy began to complain that his stomach was bad, the rice too heavy, his feet hurt, so I decided to get rid of him. I took away the bundle of rice and pointed back up the road, saying, "Mission, Mission" very firmly. He then looked really alarmed, saying "Doctor Bad, Bad".

I took it to mean that he was afraid that Robin would be angry at him for leaving me. So I got out pencil and paper and wrote a note saying he was too much trouble, pressed a rupee firmly into his hand and gave him a push in the right direction. Loogale watched all this, giving vent every now and then to distressed cries of "*Ma Ma*" but not interfering, and he made no effort to stop the boy leaving. As soon as we lost sight of him round a bend in the path, I pushed the rice into my rucksack and, with Loogale close on my heels, continued.

Loogale must have had a thing against being alone because from now on I had no more trouble with him lagging behind. Indeed, if by chance I got a bit ahead, pathetic cries of *"Ma Ma"* would ring out behind me and I would have to wait until he caught up with me again. It was just dusk when we reached the next village; the rice was weighing very heavy in my rucksack, the rain was pouring down, so it was the obvious place to spend the night.

Robin had told me that he had explained to Loogale that he would have to make the arrangements with the headmen of the villages where we would be spending the nights. Now I was anxious to see if he had understood. As soon as I told him "Sleep here," he brightened up and spoke to one of the villagers who had started crowding round. The man led the way to what, from its size, I supposed was the headman's hut. He was a cheerful little man with his head tied in a gay turquoise scarf, and he asked us into his house for a cup of tea while he sent his young daughter out to warn the family whose turn it was to accommodate travellers.

We had barely had sips of scalding hot tea before she was back, so we gathered up our stuff and followed her out and down the muddy little street to a two-storied house made of bamboo. On closer inspection it was not a two-storied house but a house on stilts. Underneath lived the pigs and chickens, separated from the kitchen quarter by a small fence; the family lived above. We climbed up a little ladder, leaving our muddy shoes on a shelf at its foot. The ladder led straight into a fair-sized room with a verandah. It had a floor of split bamboo that gave alarmingly under me. The Karens and Burmans are very slight with small, fine bones, and I must have been nearly twice their weight. As I walked on the bending floor I tried to put my feet onto that part of it that was supported on stilts from below, and, as soon as I could, I sat down. Seated I felt that my weight was much better distributed.

Various people, who did not belong to the family, had followed us in. They sat down round me and brought out their beautiful little lacquer boxes which held all the necessities for betel-nut chewing. These they offered to each other, but each person prepared their own mixture, sometimes adding a pinch of this or that out of a friend's box. They chewed all the time and spat for a lot of it; most of the spittle mercifully fell between the intersections of the floor. Only one old woman refrained, and she held her jaw tenderly in her hand, occasionally putting an exploratory finger in her mouth and moaning.

The conversation flowed on round me as I leaned comfortably back against my rucksack. Loogale was making no move to go and cook our rice. He was far too busy smoking a huge cheroot that had been pressed on him and basking in the joy of being the centre of attention. I did not bother him as I was sure that his cooking, like the rest of his work, would be of very poor quality. A woman's voice called something from below, and all the visitors got up to leave, shaking hands with me as they left.

I could now see more of my surroundings and the family I was going to spend the night with. There was a youngish man, his wife and three children, the girl who was the eldest being about 14. There was a boy of about eight and a small baby just toddling. The old woman with the bad jaw stayed, so I took her to be a grandmother.

The woman who had done the cooking now came up and was introduced, but I did not know if she was a relation or a servant. The food was not very exciting but the rice was different to any I had eaten before, being large-grained and sticky, so that we could roll it up into a sort of sausage which was easy to hold in one hand while spooning up a thin spicy soup from a communal bowl with a china spoon in the other.

The surroundings more than made up in romance what the meal lacked in nourishment. We were all seated cross-legged in a circle on the floor, dimly illuminated by some small wicks lying in little earthenware pots of oil. Curtains with appliqué work hung behind us, and two polished teak chests were against the golden bamboo walls. The light picked out the lacquer betel-nut boxes, making them glow like jewels, and shone on the neat shining hair of the women and the gaily-turbaned heads of the father and son.

The baby toddled around us as we sat, going up to different people holding his mouth open for food to be popped in. When he was thirsty he would trot round to his mother, undo her little bodice and help himself to a drink of milk.

When the meal was over we all started our preparations for bed. The mother put my things on the verandah and, just as I was getting into my bag, the old grandmother came round and, crouching down in front of me, opened her mouth, displaying a horrifying row of jet-black, worn-down teeth. She then took my hand in hers and, separating the first finger, tried to poke it down her mouth, groaning mournfully.

In Taungyi someone had told me that I would probably meet plenty of people with aching teeth and gums who, on the sight of my white face, would expect me to cure them. Oil of cloves was recommended as a kind of counter irritant, as it might possibly do some good and would certainly do no harm. This I thought would be the moment to try it, so opening my little medicine box I took out the bottle, wrapped a piece of cotton wool round a tooth-pick and soaked it in the oil of cloves. Then I told the old lady to open her mouth. By this time the whole family had stopped their preparations for bed and gathered round us, smiling and pleased. I had no idea what the result of the application would be and was not at all prepared for the strangled cry and the fearful jerk of her body as the oil saturated the tender spot.

Tears poured from her eyes and I looked apprehensively round at the rest of the family. They stood mute for a moment, and we all watched the patient anxiously as she mopped the tears from her cheeks. She put an exploratory hand to the side of her face, pressed gently, and then her mouth was split with a wide grin and she seized my hand and pressed it to her forehead, gabbling away to the rest of the family. They in turn took my hand and put it to their foreheads, smiling and thanking me.

Feeling greatly relieved I turned my attention to getting into bed. As I slipped into my sleeping bag no one paid me any attention, but when I put up my umbrella covered by the mosquito-net bag, they all burst out laughing and clustered round me again to have a better look.

I was tired and fell asleep almost instantly, only to be wakened again by an extraordinary rhythmic thumping noise from below. It was still completely dark, but I could hear the murmur of soft voices. I sat up and then realised that I had slept the night through and that dawn was breaking. The thumping was the women husking the rice for the day's food. As soon as we could see, the rest of us got up and by the time I had packed my things, the rice and soup were ready.

When I left I tried to pay for my lodging, but they would not accept any money, just smiling and patting me on the back and pressing the money back into my hand. Finally I gave them about ten pounds of my rice, killing two birds with one stone by lightening my pack and giving them at least some sort of return for their trouble.

All that day we descended and several times we had to ford fast-running little streams. The beautiful terracing had given way to casual-looking walls, and the forest was getting denser. Every now and then we would come across a section of the path that had been completely washed away or else turned into a lake through which we had to wade up to our knees. I was tired and caked in mud when at dusk we reached a village, so decided at once to stop for the night.

The headman himself put us up in the same style of house as the one we had stayed in the night before, but a little bigger and better furnished. The floor had elegant mats made of very fine woven bamboos, and we had porcelain bowls and spoons with our rice. I could recognise pieces of cooked chicken in the broth. As we sat round the food in the golden glow of the lamplight, the matting shone golden too and a couple of polished bronze dishes caught the light. The neat heads of the women above their coffee-coloured faces, made unnaturally pale by liberal applications of Thanaka powder, made a lovely peaceful picture, ruined, I felt, by my large, mud-covered figure, uncouth among the daintiness.

It was raining as we went to bed, and each time I woke up in the night I could hear the rain still falling. By the time the thump of the pestles had started, it had eased to a fine drizzle, but the headman looked serious when we left and Loogale was also upset. He lagged behind, calling in a high, dismal whine: "*Ma Ma*," every time I got too far ahead.

We were still descending slowly and we had more rain. It came down more heavily in short bursts — at least I think they were short, although they seemed to last for hours. Holding the umbrella up with both hands, because the weight of the water falling on it made it impossible for me to support it with one, I was covered with a fine spray of water that penetrated through the cotton covering. The exercise and the humidity made me sweat so much that my upper half, semi-dry from the rain, was wet with sweat, and my feet and legs were soaked with rain and covered in mud. It was really only moral support that I received from the umbrella.

This was the first day that I got leeches badly. Before, I had just found the occasional one at the end of the day, but this day as I was sitting in a miserable shed in a village waiting for tea, I started to inspect my ankles and found them encircled by a bracelet of swollen bodies. Loogale was sitting beside me, moaning softly. I thought of all the various tips I had been given about removing leeches. Some people had advocated covering them with salt, others applying lighted matches to their bottoms, and then I remembered a man who told me that by far the best thing was the sludge that the Shans had in the bottom of their pipes. This sounded to me the most attractive method, so I rounded on Loogale, who occasionally smoked a pipe, and asked him for the loan of it. After some lively pantomime, he at last understood what I wanted and handed it over.

In the bottom of the bowl, to my joy, I found a sticky sort of black gum. This I picked out with my little finger and carefully smeared over the leeches. Sure enough, they started to shrivel and drop off. I felt a little sorry for them as they dropped because I did not find them as disgusting as the other sorts of parasites due to overcrowding, and I knew that they sometimes had to wait months between meals.

By early afternoon Loogale's constant complaints and cries of "*Ma Ma*" had resulted in me taking what I felt to be at least half his load, and I was beginning to wonder how far he would actually go before he eventually gave up entirely. I thought too that his wife should really have paid me to take him away.

That night we had a sordid lodging in a very miserable village. Although the house was poor and shabby, the family were all beautifully dressed; the women's bodices starched and ironed, and both sexes in bright coloured *lungyis*. Through the night the mosquitoes hummed madly about my umbrella net, but the arrangements worked perfectly and I never got bitten while I was in bed. In spite of this sanctuary I was thankful when the thump of the rice-pounders told me that the dawn was approaching.

It was time to leave, and we said goodbye. I could see from Loogale's expression that he was hearing some bad news about our route. I shook hands firmly all round and did not even try to understand what they were telling us. I knew I would probably get it wrong and that, in any case, we had better see for ourselves what the obstacle was before deciding to give up.

Off we went, a protesting wail of *"Mas"* coming from Loogale as he followed me. This time he must have been feeling really bad because as we passed a *Nat* shrine outside the village, he gave up his pretence of being a Baptist and made offerings to the shrine in a very serious way; sprinkling rice, arranging flowers and attaching a piece of cloth which he must have brought for the purpose. He ended up prostrating himself in front of the shrine.

At first it seemed as if he had succeeded in placating the spirit. The sun came out and the path improved. Still feeling fresh, I refused to stop at the first village that we came to, but after another hour the clouds gathered and the heavens literally opened and descended on us. It was no use trying to take refuge in the dense jungle beside the path. It was far too thick to penetrate without a bush knife; besides we needed to keep moving to avoid the leeches. Loogale was partly protected by his big oiled hat, but when I looked round to see how he was getting on I could barely see him through the dense curtain of rain. He looked like a figure seen from the other side of a waterfall. I don't know how long the rain lasted, but by the time it passed I was feeling quite exhausted by the noise and strain of holding the umbrella up against the weight of water.

As soon as comparative quiet was restored, I heard the familiar cry of *"Ma Ma"*, and up tottered Loogale, crouching low and clutching his back as he gave a fine demonstration of being in great pain. This meant that I had to agree to taking a bit more of his load. We plodded on for another hour or so and then came to the edge of a river, down which was pouring a perfect torrent of water. From the satisfied look on Loogale's face I guessed that this was the obstacle that the villagers had been warning us against, and I must say it looked pretty grim.

Opposite we could see where the path carried on, but it must have been more than 100 feet across a dark-red, muddy torrent which was carrying along with it various lumps of wood and branches of trees. Obviously, given time, the river would go down, but it might take days and in the desolation all round there was no way of finding out.

We stood by the bank with even Loogale for once silent. An elderly Shan suddenly materialised beside us. He was leaning on a heavy, shoulder-length stave, and above his *lungyi* his body was completely covered with elegant tattooing. At first sight it looked as if he was wearing a close-fitting vest in a faded, cobalt-blue colour. He gestured in a friendly way at the red torrent and made motions of wading through it. I was delighted, as he was obviously the guardian of the ford, but Loogale was almost in tears. His despair reached a climax when he found out he was to be the first to cross. I am still not sure why I let him go first; whether I genuinely felt that it was better for me to be the last across or if I was subconsciously sending him out as a sort of guinea pig.

Anyway, the blue man shouldered Loogale's pack and, grasping his stave in his left hand, took Loogale's in his right. I stood on the bank watching them. After a couple of steps in the water they came to a halt and stood, heads pressed together, whispering and throwing anxious glances over their shoulders at me. At last the blue man made up his mind and, turning his back, took off his *lungyi*, disclosing two neatly tattooed blue buttocks. His *lungyi* he fastened on top of the pack. In order to spare Loogale's feelings, I ostentatiously looked the other way for about two minutes and when I turned round again they were on their way across. I could see at once that we could never have made it alone. I could, I think, have got myself across but would certainly never have been able to persuade Loogale to accompany me, and I would almost certainly have lost my footing and probably ended up swimming the last part, which would have been the ruination of the things in my rucksack.

The tattooed man held firmly onto Loogale's hand the whole way across; with his long stave he prodded before moving his feet forwards, using it like a third foot. I thought that I could hear, over the roar of the water, faint cries of *"Ma Ma"*. Twice Loogale lost his balance, to be jerked upright by the tattooed one. Eventually they reached the farther bank; Loogale tottered ashore and collapsed. Immediately the blue man, pausing only to drop the baggage — it looked to me on top of him — turned and started wading back for me.

I had taken the precaution of removing my trousers and was now ready for the crossing, dressed only in my knee-length Chinese jacket. I waded into the river, grasping the tails of my jacket in my right hand. The river gradually rose to over my knees. Finally I got to where modesty forbade me to lift the jacket any higher and I waited till the blue man approached to within three yards. There he stood still and beckoned me towards him.

Unwilling to lift my clothes any higher, I beckoned him towards me. He shook his head and for a moment we faced each other, bending forwards, hands outstretched to their fullest extent but still failing to meet. He beckoned me, I beckoned him, and we lent so far towards each other that we nearly overbalanced, and it was not till I saw his spare hand descend to cover his genitals that I realised he was even more handicapped than me, as, except for the tattooing and the water, he was completely naked. So, taking pity on him, I advanced.

He grasped my hand and together we crossed. I was very glad he was there; the water was running at a tremendous pace, and in the river-bed stones and boulders were being rolled down by the water. They made a loud grumbling noise and could have damaged our legs badly unless we were nippy at getting out of their way. I felt quite a sense of achievement by the time we were across.

Loogale greeted me as if I had arrived across Niagara Falls in a barrel. I gave the tattooed man some money, with which he seemed inordinately pleased, and then we started on again. By this time I was convinced that I must be carrying everything I possessed. Loogale was carrying his own stuff and he looked as if he had as much as me. I decided that as soon as we got to the Catholic mission, which I thought must be quite near now, I would get rid of him. I had not liked to do it before, as there was going to be a good deal of working out about the money I had paid his wife in advance. Since he had not even half fulfilled his contract, there was really nothing due to him, but at the same time I could not send him back with no money for his journey. It would all have to be explained through an interpreter.

As we went on, my hopes rose that we were getting to the right village. The path gradually broadened and became smoother, and I noticed a few side-tracks coming in to join it. When we rounded the next bend we saw the beginnings of a village and then, as the country spread out before us, I noticed the steeple of a church. I took the first path leading in its direction, and as we got nearer we saw that it was in a walled compound with some other buildings where there was a lot of work going on. The church itself was being added to and so was the wall. Due to the weather and the work, the whole compound was a sea of mud. As I passed through the gate, Loogale burst into a staggering run and caught hold of my sleeve, trying to stop me from entering and crying, "No, No, Catholic," with an expression of absolute horror on his face.

I pressed on remorselessly with him clinging to my arm in a perfectly ridiculous manner. My head was down and I was staggering with exhaustion, augmented by the weight of my rucksack and the drag of the wretched Loogale. Suddenly I saw a pair of muddy grey flannel trousers approaching and I could hardly believe that I heard English being spoken. Not very well, it is true, but easily understandable. I came to an abrupt halt and saw standing in front of me a young bearded man wearing a beret above a whitish shirt and grey flannels. He was holding out his hand.

"I am Father Ignacio, head of this mission," he said. "Is there anything I can do to help you?"

"Oh, thank you so much. That is why I have come, to ask your help. I am Beryl Boxer on my way to Chieng Mai."

"Well, let us get into shelter," he said quickly, "it is going to rain again."

He led the way into a small temporary shelter and I sat down gratefully on an upturned wooden box. Loogale had disappeared as soon as Father Ignacio spoke to me. I had no idea where he had gone and did not care at all.

Father Ignacio had a thin, aesthetic face. At first he seemed to be a true martyr type, but when I looked at him again I caught him regarding me with a quizzical unmartyr-like look, which, as I proceeded with my story, turned into open laughter.

"It's Loogale who has really brought me to you," I finished up. "I simply cannot stand that awful whine of '*Ma Ma*' any more, and as you saw, I am carrying all my own stuff anyway. Please will you sack him for me?"

"Well, that isn't going to be too simple either. It will be difficult to persuade him that a Catholic could speak the truth, but we can try. Also, what will you do without him?"

"I will be able to manage by myself; the villagers have always been so kind and friendly, and the path seems pretty straightforward. Even if it is bad, it's better than the other tracks that join it, so I think I could always recognise it. Now that I am carrying all the stuff it would mean that I would have to go a bit slower."

He looked thoughtful over this but did not say any more. The rain stopped as suddenly as it had started, and he went to the doorway and shouted. There was a distant cry in answer, and in a minute or two Loogale appeared at the door, escorted by another Burman. They did not look as if they cared particularly for each other's company. Father Ignacio addressed Loogale in a rush of Burmese. Loogale looked taken aback and bleated "*Ma Ma*" in a very depressed manner, then replied more fully to Father Ignacio. After a few more exchanges the father said to me, "He will not believe that you want him to leave. He says that Mr. Kirkman told him he was to take you to the road and he thinks that I am just trying to get rid of him so that I can get you to employ a Catholic instead. You must stand up beside me and speak very slowly in English saying that you want him to leave and that you will give him a note to Mr. Kirkman saying why you want him to leave. Stop after each sentence for me to translate and be sure to nod your head in an approving manner each time I pause. Then he will see that you think I am interpreting your remarks correctly."

There we stood solemnly, side by side, while Loogale regarded us apprehensively. He was really quite good and made no trouble when we got on to the money arrangements, being quite happy to leave with three rupees. He had not at all enjoyed his trip and was obviously longing to get away from the mission before the devil himself, wearing horns and a tail, arrived to devour him. As soon as I had written the note to Robin Kirkman, he almost snatched it from my hand and bolted off down the drive as if pursued by demons.

"The poor man," said Father Ignacio rather complacently as he watched the retreating figure, "he really is frightened of us."

In spite of the heat, the mud, the humidity and the prospect of carrying my load for another hundred-odd miles, I felt a blissful sense of release. No longer would I be plagued by those wails of "*Ma Ma*" and that constant look of misery, Loogale's characteristic expression no matter what kind of suggestion I was trying to make. I turned to Father Ignacio. "Thank you so much; I feel a new woman to be on my own at last."

Father Ignacio looked as if he took this remark with a pinch of salt, then he tentatively tried my rucksack.

"Perhaps," he said with a laugh,"you will be missing him in a day or two. I might be able to find someone here who would go with you."

"Dr. Kirkman said that the proper coolies won't travel in the monsoon and that in any event they are not accustomed to just going alone, that they prefer to travel in a group and feed and sleep together. That is why Loogale was the best he could do. After him I don't want to try another amateur."

He walked over to the door and stood there leaning against a post. He looked very thin and tired. He was watching the men working on the building of the church. Suddenly he straightened up and turned round with a smile.

"I've got it. How do you feel about the Chinese?"

"I am absolutely mad about them. Why? Do you mean that you know a Chinese who might come with me? Oh, that would be too wonderful." I looked at him anxiously; it seemed altogether too much luck in one day to get rid of Loogale and then to find a Chinese.

"That is just what I do mean. He is not a coolie but he is a good carpenter and he has worked on and off for me for two years now. At the moment there is not much need for him until the builders have done a bit more. I could let him go for about two weeks or more, which should give him plenty of time to take you to the bus road and get back again. As long as I guaranteed to take him back, I think he would like to go. He is rather a restless type and has been working steadily for a few months already. Anyway, we can ask him and see what he says."

After a few minutes, up walked a short, thickset Chinese wearing a straw hat and blue cotton trousers fastened low round his hips and rolled up to just above his knees. His round, light-brown face wore a friendly, open smile and his eyes flickered enquiringly from Father Ignacio's face and then to mine. I felt with that flash of intuition that comes occasionally on meeting strangers, "He will come with me."

Father Ignacio started explanations to Ah Kee, who listened silently; then when the father had finished, he asked some questions which the father answered quickly, not referring to me. When they had finished talking, he turned to me and said, "He says he would like to go with you. I have guaranteed to take him back even if he does take longer than two weeks. He is asking a stiff price but you will have to pay him carpenter's wages, of course, since that is his real trade. Also he knows you are stuck. He says he will fix up to see that you have accommodation each night and will see to the morning and evening meal for both of you. Anything you need while on the road will be extra, but I think he will be worth it. He is asking three rupees a day all-in. He also wants to know if you will eat Burmese food?"

"Of course, I will gladly pay him that, but how does he want it? I have only 40 rupees on me, so I could give him 12 now which will be enough for four days."

There was more conversation and then Father Ignacio said, "Give him 12 now. He will go and make his arrangements and says he will be back and ready to start in two hours. He is going to take a little rice in case you get stuck between villages. He wants to do longer than normal stages. He knows the road well, as that is the way he always comes from China."

Ah Kee and I now solemnly shook hands to seal our bargain, and I gave him 12 rupees. He went off briskly, quite unlike the miserable shamble Loogale had accustomed me to.

"Now you must come to the mission and have a glass of wine. I am sorry not to have offered it to you before."

"But you have already given me the best present I have ever had. This next part of the trip is going to be wonderful, and I can't wait to get started."

He laughed and then smiled at me. "Well, you will have to wait at least two hours, so you can have a glass of wine and meet the Mother Superior who runs the orphanage. I know she and the sisters will want you to lunch with them before you leave. We seldom have visitors and never ladies."

He led the way to a small hut, very poorly furnished and without any comfort at all. We sat down carefully on two unsteady-looking chairs beside a rickety table, and a young Burman brought us two glasses of surprisingly good wine. I had never before met a priest who had no exterior sign of his calling and found it hard to remember that this tired-looking young man in old grey flannel trousers and a dirty shirt was the priest of a large parish.

If anything, I belong to the Church of England and really consider that all non-conformist religions come, more or less, under the same heading. I chattered away with all the fluency of a person who has not spoken their own language or seen a person of their own race for nearly a week. I constantly found caustic remarks about some non-Catholic missionary effort popping out and only remembered who I was speaking to when I saw the smile on his face.

As we sat talking, a young Burman girl came up and spoke to Father Ignacio. He turned to me, getting to his feet as he spoke.

"She comes from the Mother Superior who wants me to take you over to see her and meet the sisters. It was wrong of me to keep you talking so long; they have far fewer visitors than I."

The rain was falling in torrents again as we walked across the muddy compound under my umbrella.

"I am afraid you will have an uncomfortable journey on from here," he said. "This is about the rainiest part of the season and it will get worse as you go down to Siam."

We passed through a door in a long wall and found ourselves in what must have been, in the dry season, a pretty garden but was now a riot of overgrown vegetation. There was a long, white-washed building, looking a bit damp, and in its doorway was standing the Mother Superior, wreathed in smiles and dressed in a spotless white habit. She seized my hand in both of hers and, speaking quite good English, drew me indoors, saying, "Come in, come in, it is such a pleasure for us to see another woman here. Can you spend at least tonight with us?"

I started to excuse myself, feeling rather boorish, but luckily Father Ignacio came to my rescue.

"No," he said firmly, "she must leave at once after lunch as Ah Kee is going with her and I want him back as soon as possible."

"Come over to my hut before you leave," he said to me. "Ah Kee will be there and we can make all arrangements perfectly clear before you start."

The nuns' home was delightful. It too showed signs of poverty, but it was gaily painted and spotlessly clean, and bright flowers below the pictures of saints distracted attention from the paucity of furniture. The nuns came in smiling and were introduced. They were all Italian — one middle-aged and two young ones. Lunch was ready and we went straight to the little dining-room where we had a completely Italian meal; spaghetti and tomatoes with salad and Chianti, though I think that the Chianti was just in my honour.

Only the Mother Superior spoke English, the others speaking in Italian and the local Shan dialect, but it was a gay meal and they were all thrilled to find that I had travelled in Italy and had actually visited the small town and a village which were the homes of two of them.

After lunch the youngest and prettiest nun took me round the orphanage. By this time we could understand each other quite

well in a mixture of English, French and Italian, and she questioned me eagerly about Ventimiglia, which was her home.
"How long have you been here?" I asked, looking at her lovely fresh pink cheeks.
"Six months."
"When do you go home again?"
"Never," she cried passionately, then suddenly bent to pick up one of the enchanting little children who were crowding round us, and holding her tight in her arms, kissed her gently and said, "It is worth it to help these little ones; it is worth it."

CHAPTER THIRTEEN
INTO SIAM

A T two o'clock I was back at Father Ignacio's hut, and in a few minutes we were joined by Ah Kee. He was wearing a large oiled-straw hat and a pair of very tatty shorts, and although he had a fair-sized bundle of his own, he took everything of mine as well. I was left with only my umbrella and the Shan bag to carry. Father Ignacio arranged that Ah Kee would be responsible for getting the food, and I agreed to eat what he produced and not to expect European-style food. We both shook hands with Father Ignacio, but when I tried to thank him for letting me have Ah Kee, he interrupted me, saying, "I do need him, as you guessed, but I have noticed lately that he was getting restless, which means that he might go off on his own any day now, in which case I never know when he will come back. Now I am almost certain that he will be back in two weeks and then he might settle down for another three months."

We set off at a good brisk pace and in no time had left all signs of human occupation behind. We were walking along a narrow mud path through such dense green jungle that it would have been impossible to leave the track unless we had used a knife to cut the creepers that laced the trees together. It was hot and airless, and we walked along drenched in sweat. When not drenched by rain I found that I used my umbrella more as a walking-stick to stop myself slipping in the sticky mud than as a protection from the rain. It was a temptation to roll up my long trousers to try to get cooler, but the sight of Ah Kee's tick-covered

147

legs stopped me from doing so. We walked along steadily all afternoon. Now that I was not weighed down by my rucksack I felt in the mood for conversation so tried talking to Ah Kee. I could remember a few basic words of Chinese that I had learnt on a visit to China. Then there were my few words of Shan that I had learnt for Loogale. Ah Kee himself knew a few words of English, so between us, given time, we could make a little sense.

He seemed to have travelled a lot, and I came to the conclusion that he was probably a part-time smuggler. There could be no reason for him to take such a long way round from Burma to China if he really travelled, as Father Ignacio said, always via Siam. His large pack became filled in my imagination with all sorts of illicit goods like opium and precious stones. If he really was a smuggler, working as my coolie would probably be a great help to him for getting across the border. Perhaps his spells of carpentry at the Catholic mission were to pass the time till the authorities had forgotten him.

With all these attempts at conversation and my speculations, the afternoon flashed by and I was surprised to find it was getting dusk. As I was wondering how much farther we would have to go, we came out of the forest to some cleared land and I saw ahead the glow of a light. Ah Kee motioned me to go on ahead and, thinking that he just wanted to relieve himself, I walked slowly on. Just as I was entering the little village I heard hurried steps behind me and, turning round, saw to my surprise an absolutely new Ah Kee. He was now wearing a beautifully pressed, cream-coloured shantung suit with the little stand-up collar, frogged buttonholes and the three-quarter-length trousers of the Chinese. He looked elegant beyond belief and laughed with pleasure at my admiration and surprise. He led me to a small tea shelter and ordered tea, then disappeared.

He was gone only a few minutes and a crowd barely had time to gather before he was back again. Smiling and telling me to follow him, he took me to a fair-sized bamboo hut. It was the same design as the others I had stayed in but the kitchen was upstairs. I walked carefully over the floor, which swayed and groaned as I stepped on it.

The owners greeted me warmly and it looked as if they were old friends of Ah Kee's. As soon as he had seen me comfortably settled, he crossed over to the kitchen and crouched down beside the lady of the house who was cooking the meal. That evening we had a splendid dinner, which I am sure was largely due to Ah Kee's culinary efforts, and for the first time I had brown rice and thought it as superior to white rice as brown bread is to white.

I lay down to sleep without a care in the world. With Ah Kee in control I had nothing to worry about. I felt that whatever might turn up — flooded rivers, broken bridges or awkward frontier guards, for I had no visas for Siam — Ah Kee would be able to cope.

I had the best night I had had since leaving Kentung and woke up to find Ah Kee already up and making me a cup of tea. While I sipped it, he rolled up my bedding and packed it away in my rucksack. He had even managed to dry my clothes, and it was lovely to put on dry clothes even when I knew that before long they would be wet for the rest of the day.

We got off in good time and went on at the same brisk pace as before. I saw now why Ah Kee had guaranteed to be back in two weeks. Carrying a load, I could not possibly have walked so fast. Ah Kee was just wearing his shorts and had at the start, but when about midday we were approaching a village, he again made me go on while he effected his transformation.

We stopped at a tea shelter and ordered some food. It was the first time that I had realised that these little places could provide food, and while we ate, the crowd gathered. They squatted in a circle round us a little distance off, smoked, chewed betel nut and discussed, I suppose, me or foreigners in general. Fewer people now were dressed in the colourful Burmese style. Most of them had gone over to the dull black of the Siamese. The children, who depended on their mother's milk for about their first three years, would trot about going to their mothers to help themselves when thirsty. Sometimes if a mother did not want to be bothered, she would offer the child a pull at her cheroot, which appeared to be a very satisfactory substitute. I did not see any small children chewing betel nut, but I was always offered some, and as long as I was sitting out of doors I enjoyed chewing it and spitting. Indoors I always had to refuse it, as I could never bring myself to spit on the floor.

About five minutes after we left the village, Ah Kee dropped behind to change back into his tatty old shorts. Now even in the rain I was thoroughly enjoying myself. In between the villages we seemed to be the only people on the road; a good thing as the path was bad enough with just us on it. If there had been any more traffic, particularly with animals, it would have been almost impossible. Our main delays were caused by flooded rivers. Ah Kee always carried out a most careful survey before attempting to cross.

In the late afternoon Ah Kee started to try to tell me something about the village where he was planning to spend the night. At first I could not understand what he was getting at. "Tonight" I understood well enough, but then he started saying something about the people of the village. I knew the word for "bad", but that was not what he meant, and at last after a good deal of pantomime I realised he was saying "ill" or "sick". I mumbled after him, "People all sick", in a wondering tone of voice, when suddenly my mind flashed back to Kentung and Robin saying, "You must try not to stay at one village; they are all lepers there."

I looked at Ah Kee with horror. "Like this?" I asked, going into a pantomime of being without fingers or toes. He broke into a beaming smile at this surprising proof of my intelligence. "Yes, yes," he said happily, "all village sick."

"Let us go on to the next village," I suggested, but he was dead against that and as for the idea of camping, leprosy itself, I felt at that moment, would almost be better.

We were plodding through dense jungle and the rain was pouring remorselessly down. Ah Kee was absolutely festooned with leeches and I was well decorated with them myself. So I tried to think of all the stories I had heard, or read, of doctors, priests and nuns who had lived for years among lepers without getting leprosy, and gradually managed to convince myself there would be no danger.

It was dusk when we arrived at the village, and it looked, I thought, rather superior to the healthy villages we had passed; the houses looked larger and better built. The only curious thing was the way the people paid absolutely no attention to us; not even a child came to stare.

Ah Kee said that there was a house for travellers kept up by the villagers and we would go straight there. He led the way to a very fine wooden house in the middle of an open space at the far end of the village. It was already lit up, and I could see shadows of people moving about inside and hear a noise going on. I followed him up some wooden steps and across a wide verandah supported on big teak logs and painted blood-red. We came then into a large room with an alcove curtained off by a rich silk-and-gold hanging. The whole place was permeated by a strong smell of decay.

A small oil lamp gave a golden glow to the wooden walls and picked out the gold threads in the rich silk *lungyi* of a man who was standing in one corner of the room by what at first sight I took to be a bundle of old clothes. Then I realised that a curious mumbling noise that I had been hearing for a little while was coming from the bundle. I moved nearer to see what it was.

Lying on the floor and looking as if she was already dead, for she was plainly decomposing, was a woman, her age impossible to determine. She was quite well-dressed and she was making the noise. As I drew nearer I realised she was also the source of the smell of decay. Ah Kee joined me and together we stood silent beside the man. It was with a feeling of relief that I saw she was long past any help I might have been able to offer. It looked to me as if she would die any minute, and my only thought was the sooner the better.

As we all stood quietly, there came a found of footsteps and the tinkle of a bell. Up the stairs came a priest with his acolyte carrying various little bronze dishes and a water container. These he proceeded to arrange round the woman. He also lit some sticks of incense which were a great help against the smell.

One of the men following the priest got into a whispered conversation with Ah Kee and then they walked across to another curtain and, when I followed them, he ushered us both inside. We were now in another curtained-off area about the size of a hall. There was a pile of sleeping mats in one corner and in an alcove was a big earthenware jar filled with fresh water for washing. But in spite of all these facilities I was determined to leave, and to my joy I saw that Ah Kee was not too happy either.

"This is the rest-house," he explained to me, "but as not travellers in monsoon they bring sick woman when she start smell. She go tonight," he added with a meaningful look.

"Bad house," I answered. "You find better place. I not sleep here."

He may not have understood all I said but he certainly got the gist of it. We went back to the other room where there was now quite an orchestra squatting round the poor woman, plucking at the strings of their instruments, but it was enough to cover her mumbling as the incense had covered the smell.

Ah Kee picked up our bundles and we slipped quietly out. Outside it was pitch dark, the street only marked by the lights showing through the walls of the houses on either side. Ah Kee went along as if he knew where he was going and in a few minutes turned into a house on the right-hand side of the street. I waited outside, thinking it would be better for him to make the arrangements before the owners saw me in case they did not want a foreigner. He came back in a few minutes, saying, "Good people, not sick," which I hoped meant that they did not have leprosy.

The house was the best-built one that I had stayed in since leaving Kentung and had the same scheme of partitions by curtains as the rest-house had had, but now they were all drawn back and it gave a wonderful sense of cool space. There were three bronze lamps, and in one corner of the room was a loom with an unfinished, brightly coloured piece of material on it. It was altogether a much more solid and permanent sort of building, though not on such a grand scale as the rest-house, and I wondered why the leper village should have such a bourgeois air.

The family, though kind and hospitable, lacked the happy, carefree manner that all the Shans and Burmans had. The faces of the father and mother carried an anxious look even in repose. I was feeling tired with the long day that we had had, culminating in the dreadful death scene, and as soon as the evening's rice was eaten, this time without any little embellishments by Ah Kee, I stepped out on the verandah where I had seen Ah Kee put my rucksack. I found that he had arranged my sleeping bag, pyjamas and umbrella, and in no time I was asleep.

In the morning we were up early, both of us anxious to leave the village. As we walked along, I wished that I could have kept Ah Kee with me; with him I could have walked across Siam to Angkor and not have had to take buses and trains, but he only had two weeks and Father Ignacio needed him, so I had to push the temptation out of my mind.

Each night when we stopped in the villages, he went to houses where he was known and, as far as I could judge, they were always owned by one of the wealthiest of the villagers. He would take up his position by the cook and nearly always managed to add some tasty Chinese dish to the rather dull Burmese food and always without arousing any resentment. Whenever I admired any particular dish that accompanied the evening rice, it was always one that Ah Kee had been responsible for. But however dull the side dishes were, the rice itself was delicious and in such variety too. The brown rice always remained my favourite. The glutinous white rice had a nice flavour but I could not take to its stickiness.

We must have been doing sometimes 25 miles a day and I have no idea when we crossed the border, but I knew we were across when we came to a village with proper little shops and a proper tea house. We had almost imperceptibly been edging out of the really dense forest, and just before getting to the village we had joined a track wide enough for bullock-carts. There was a small inn, surprisingly clean, though that may have been due to the fact that there was nothing to get dirty, the rooms consisting as they did of four walls and a mat. That night I had for the first time the national dish of pink rice, looking most attractive, although the taste was identical with the white rice. The savoury dishes served with it seemed to be chosen with an eye to appearance as well as taste.

I was depressed that night as I fought my way into my umbrella net through a dense cloud of virulent mosquitoes. The stagnant water which lay everywhere provided perfect hatcheries for them. I knew also that next day we would be arriving at Chieng Mai, and after that it would be just the train to Bangkok. I have never cared for capital cities.

The Siamese rulers, when they decided to modernise their country, went about it in an original way. They built either a good modern road or else a railway, but there was never any choice. The only way south was by rail.

In the morning we took things easily; we dawdled over our tea and it was well after sunrise when we got going. We left by the same bullock-cart track as we had come in by the night before. As we went along, Ah Kee told me that by midday we should get to a small town where there was a bus service to Chieng Mai. We trudged slowly along until we sighted the town and Ah Kee slipped off to put on his good suit. As we got in among the crowds and threaded our way through the crowded street, I felt dazed and foolish and found myself gaping at the most ordinary things hung up in the shops. I had to curb my tendency to stand and stare, entranced, at a man winding up a gramophone with a horn. Ah

Kee was much more blasé and hurried me along to a ramshackle building with the word "Otel" painted on it in large green letters. He left me there with the baggage while he went off to find out about the bus.

When he came back he had two tickets in his hand for seats on the bus leaving that afternoon. We had lunch with more pink rice and then walked to the bus stop. The bus from the outside looked quite smart, but it took two men 15 minutes to start it, and some heart-rending groans came from the engine as they worked.

As usual Ah Kee had fixed us up in style. We had the two good seats next to the driver, while behind us people were jammed in, some standing and others on their relations' laps. When the last duck was secured, the bus set off along a road that not only looked good but felt good too. It was evening when we reached Chieng Mai and Ah Kee took me to an hotel that was of a depressingly standard type, with beds, sheets, dressing-table and bathroom, and a dining-room with imitation European food which made me yearn for pink rice. Ah Kee had left me, once he had seen me properly installed, saying that he would come back in the morning.

Next morning I put on my dress, which, after having made the journey in the bottom of my rucksack, was a bit the worse for wear in spite of a thorough pressing. However, when Ah Kee arrived in his smart suit, I felt, sartorially speaking, on level terms with him. We went to the bank and then to the station.

At the station we were told that there was a train leaving that evening; the first for a few days as a bad flood had washed away a section of the line. The train due to leave that evening would go as far as the wash-out, then the passengers would have to disembark and walk across the wash-out to a train that would be waiting on the other side.

I was appalled at my own reaction to this news. Ah Kee had ruined me; I was no longer the intrepid woman who had contemplated, undismayed, the prospect of walking a hundred-odd miles through the monsoon carrying her own pack. Now the idea of a train trip to Bangkok, with a portage across a wash-out and without Ah Kee to help me, filled me with alarm.

We walked back to the town and had lunch, and then I paid Ah Kee. After he had thanked me and pocketed the money, he said he would come back to the hotel at four o'clock and take me to the station to be sure that I got a seat on the train.

So at four o'clock Ah Kee and I, followed by a boy carrying my luggage, started off to the station. We stopped at a road-side eating house and had some pink rice. When we got to the station there was an enormous crowd. It seemed impossible that they were all intending to travel, but most of them were, and without Ah Kee I should never have got a seat. He hurled himself into the scrum round the train and appeared a few minutes later at one of the windows. I passed him my rucksack and then forced myself into the carriage to find he had got me a corner seat.

We then said goodbye and he climbed out of the window very carefully so as not to dirty his suit. Back on the platform he straightened his coat, smoothed down his trousers, turned to smile at me, bowed and was gone.

CHAPTER FOURTEEN
THE COMING OF WAR

THE train was so crowded that I had almost as much as I could do to breathe, pressed in as I was from front and side. What made matters worse was that no one had troubled to stow their luggage properly, the wash-out not being very far away. With every jolt the train gave as it ran along the storm-weakened track, bundles and baskets crashed down on our heads. It was quite dark when we got to the wash-out but everybody tumbled out laughing and shouting, as if it was a perfect treat to have to change trains in the middle of the night.

In fact it was quite fun and not nearly as wet and slippery as the paths I had been using in Burma. The train we transferred to was far larger than the one from Chieng Mai. It was a corridor train too, which surprised me and made it much easier to find a seat. The carriages were not quite as clean and roomy as the Burmese ones, and the people, though friendly, were much plainer-looking and their clothes less colourful. The women in particular had a drabber and more harried air. There was a restaurant-car serving only pink rice, and by the time the train reached Bangkok I was feeling quite adjusted to civilisation.

In spite of my dislike of capitals, Bangkok had such a merry kind of charm that I was quite taken with it but did not spend much time there. Now I was back in a place where I could hear the news by radio. The situation in Europe, which I had almost totally forgotten for the past month or so, was worse than ever. I decided to push on to Angkor as it would probably be the only chance I would ever have of seeing it and, in the unlikely event of the war not breaking out, I would be that much farther on my way to Hong Kong and Canada.

I had found that above the station there was a row of bedrooms to let. They looked quite clean, had running water and were extremely cheap. I took one and found a charming notice discreetly pinned behind the door saying, "Visitors are forbidden in these rooms after 11 p.m. but if the occupant wishes a friend to stay the night, the management should be notified and a fee of two shillings will be charged."

To get on to Angkor, which was at that time in French Indo-China, I had to take a train to a station near the Siamese frontier. From there a bus ran to the French frontier where I would have to change into another bus that ran to Siemreap, the small town nearest the ruins. Two days after arriving in Bangkok I was on a train, travelling third class as usual, on my way to the frontier. It was not such a long journey as the one from Chieng Mai but infinitely more leisurely. The train stopped for ten to 15 minutes at the stations while the passengers got down and walked about, buying food, tea and soft drinks. On some stations the vendors looked as if they far outnumbered the passengers.

There were only two other Europeans besides me on the train and they were travelling second class. One was an elderly, grey-haired, slow-moving man, with a tanned, leathery face and the large horny hands of a seaman or farm labourer. He looked a little lost among the svelte and sprightly Siamese. The other was tall, dark and suave, good-looking and wearing a clergyman's collar. At about the fourth stop he came up and spoke to me in excellent English. He said he was a Jesuit priest returning to Saigon via Angkor and that he had heard there might be trouble at the frontier because of the threat of war, and he offered to help me if there was, as he was French himself.

By the time we came to the terminus, the train was practically empty; only about six Siamese were left and we three Europeans. There was a bus standing waiting and we all got in. I found myself sitting next to the elderly man. He spoke to me in the most amazingly garbled English, and I could hardly understand a word but thought that it sounded from his accent as if he might be German. I asked him, "*Sprechen sie Deutsch?*" His whole face lit up and he seized me by the hand, shaking it warmly and giving it tremendous squeezes while he volleyed questions at me about transport in Indo-China and the possibilities of war in general. I could only tell him that I really knew no more about the situation than he did but that the Jesuit priest, who was French, had offered to help us if there was any difficulty at the border.

As the bus drove through the flat, green, cultivated land, Herr Grunther told me his story. He was in fact an American citizen, having emigrated to the States 40 years before, and had gone directly to Alaska where he had stayed ever since, living, apparently, from the state of his English, entirely among Germans. Somehow — he was not very clear about it — he had become very rich and, on getting ill, had been advised by the doctor to take a sea voyage. He did this but had not enjoyed shipboard life. One of his fellow travellers had suggested, when he complained about being bored, that he pay a visit to Angkor and that was what he was doing.

While he was talking, the bus slowed down and stopped at a bamboo pole placed across the road. Out of a bamboo hut beside it came three officials. They did not seem particularly interested in us three Europeans but questioned the other passengers, several of whom were made to get out. Then one of the officials removed the bamboo, and the bus, by this time with only six of us inside, moved on.

The French side of the frontier was only a few hundred yards away but it was much more official-looking; a couple of well-built huts with wooden doors and window frames, and several soldiers with guns. Inside one hut was the immigration man, sitting at a table with plenty of paper forms on it and even a pot of that ghastly purplish ink that congeals slowly in all French post offices. Behind him stood a small group of grim-looking officials, and at first it looked as if none of us were going to pass. It was quite obvious from our reception that we were not wanted. Curiously, the French Jesuit seemed as unwelcome as the rest of us and, before he could be any help as an interceder, he was whisked off into another room. The Siamese, if they were Siamese, got short shrift too. Finally there was only a very old man, Herr Grunther and me left. Herr Grunther's method of coping was to sit in a chair and reply to whatever question was asked, "United States citizen," and tap the table-top with his passport. I tried to appeal to French gallantry, and no one paid the slightest attention to the old man.

At last the man I was importuning gave me a grudging permission to cross and stamped my passport. As he stood there for a moment, Herr Grunther, with surprising smartness, slipped his open passport down on the table just under the stamp, saying firmly, "United States citizen," and the Frenchman meekly stamped it, too.

While this was going on, another bus had come in from the French side, also with only a few passengers, who now stood dejectedly outside in the sun. Herr Grunther and I hurried into the newly arrived bus and sat down; the old man followed us. We waited apprehensively in case the French might change their minds, and sounds of argument came streaming out from the hut. Suddenly, a door at the back burst open and the driver appeared, arguing with an official, who was holding on to him with one hand. Finally he broke away and came rushing over to the bus, jumped in and pressed the self-starter, while he still shouted at the official who confined himself to shaking his fist. We moved off as if we were going to mow down anyone rash enough to stand in the way.

There was, of course, no change in the scenery or passers-by after we had crossed the border and we ran on, stopping now and then to pick up the odd passenger, until we came to the big hotel built for tourists visiting the ruins. It was an enormous pile of gloomy grey masonry and particularly dismal, as it was only half open because of the monsoon. Herr Grunther had sent them a telegram, so he was expected; I stayed in the bus which was going on to the small town of Siemreap to stay at the hotel there as I thought it would not only be cheaper but not so touristy either. Although an ardent tourist myself, I always have an irrational fear of being taken for one.

The bus went on for about three miles and then entered a pretty town with a canal running through it, bordered by grass and flowering bushes. Big trees shaded the road. The bus stopped near a one-storied building and the driver said that it was the hotel. I got out with my baggage, and a servant came out of the hotel. He took it from me and led me into the lobby. There was no one there but I could hear the sounds of a radio being twiddled, and above its anguished shrieks I could hear the sound of men's voices. The servant came back followed by the French manager who asked me to sign the register. As he saw me write down the word English, he smiled. "Come quickly," he said in French, "the news is very bad and we cannot get the Saigon radio, only sometimes the B.B.C. and that we cannot understand. You must translate for us."

Seizing me by the arm he rushed me into the room where the radio was. He went straight up to it, taking me with him. "An English woman; quick, quick, the B.B.C." he said. An immediate hush fell. For a minute there was just the faint squeak as he gently turned the dial, then suddenly there was a burst of static and I could hear an English voice. I bent my head nearer the radio; the voice came stronger.

"This morning," it said, "the Germans crossed the frontier into Poland. Intense fighting is going on."

It faded again in another burst of static. The Frenchmen crowded round me with anxious looks. As I told them what I had been able to hear, they fell silent. "Now it will start again," said one older man with a sigh, and another asked me if I thought that this time the English would fight.

"Yes," I said, "this time she has promised." They looked at me sadly; it was clear that they would have liked me to have been a bit doubtful. I left the room quickly — I felt that at this time they would not want a foreigner — and went to my room.

The hotel was small and crowded; planters from miles round had come in to hear the news. Radios were not so common then and not all of them had them on their plantations. After my bath, when I went down again, they welcomed me and made me join their circle on the hotel verandah. As I listened to them talking, I was struck by the fact that their great fear was the reaction among the local population. It was that which was worrying them far more than the fact that France would be at war in Europe.

They were nearly all men of military age and would be called up to join some branch of the services, and they were appalled at the idea of leaving their families alone, being convinced that their lives would be in danger from attacks by the Indo-Chinese. I found this outlook very surprising. It seemed queer that India, with its teeming population and its terrible poverty, should be kinder to the white man than these people with a far higher standard of living.

Next morning there was still no declaration of war and the French began to regain some of their gaiety, but I persisted in my belief that England would fight so made enquiries about getting back to Bangkok. There was no bus before September 4th, but it was already the 2nd so that did not mean much delay. I bought my ticket and reserved a seat next to the driver, then decided to hire a bicycle to see as much of the ruins of Angkor Wat as I could. I could only get a man's bicycle and it was one of those high-seated, low-handle affairs that the French prefer, and on it I set off to visit the ruins.

The weather was damp, sultry and oppressive, as if the war clouds in Europe were pressing down out here, nearly half a world away. As I biked and walked alone among the ruins I was filled with despair. Did this war mean the end of our civilisation? And, if so, what lovely ruins would survive from it for future generations to visit? I could think of nothing made in this century that could compare with these Khmer ruins. Almost the only durable buildings that I could think of were the Menin Gate and the war graves.

All that day as I walked and biked, pushing my way through dense and dripping vegetation to find some little shrine, the only signs of life I saw were water buffaloes, birds and, in any ruin boasting a corridor, bats.

When I got back to the hotel that evening there was a much more cheerful feeling, as there was still no declaration of war. Next morning I was up and out early to get the hottest part of my ride over while it was still cool. This time I took a map I had been given of the ruins and conscientiously visited every insignificant site marked. Although it was not the type of beauty that really appeals to me, as I like stark ruins and treeless landscapes, it was the loneliness, the feeling of something hidden and mysterious, that kept drawing me from site to site. Each time I penetrated into some bat-filled, dank, dark corridor, I was expecting to find some marvel, but of course I never did.

That evening when I got back, the war had been officially declared and the bar was full of men discussing anxiously what arrangements they could make for the safety of their families. They all pressed me to join them in drinking to our countries' alliance, but I left as soon as I could, thinking of my early start in the morning and being ravenous after the day's sightseeing.

I had just got started on my dinner when in walked the Jesuit priest who had been on the train. He came and sat down with me but brushed off my enquiries as to why he had been delayed at the frontier.

"What are your plans now?" he asked. "The French will close all the borders soon."

"I am going back to Bangkok by bus tomorrow; I took a seat on the early morning one."

"Well," he said, with, I thought, a certain amount of relish. "You will have a long delay at the frontier. Yesterday they were searching everything; even books they were inspecting, page by page; and money, they will take it all."

If it had not been for the excellent bottle of wine he had ordered and the good liqueur brandy at the end of the meal, I might have been quite cast down by all his prognostications. However, when I was back in my room I looked through all my things to see if there was anything that might upset a suspicious frontier guard. All I could find was my marriage certificate. I felt they might legitimately wonder why I should choose to travel under my maiden name, but I was loath to destroy it so folded it very small and put it in my pocket, thinking I might try to swallow it, as I had heard that that was what missionaries in China always did with their wedding rings when captured by bandits.

As I crept down the darkened corridor at four o'clock in the morning, a door opened and out popped the priest.

"Goodbye and good luck," he whispered, "courage, courage," making me feel as if I was going into battle instead of a bus.

The bus was waiting and empty. We drove down to the town proper after I had got in but there were only three other passengers. We had a quick drive to the frontier and my heart sank when I saw the grim faces of the officials who were waiting for us.

As I stepped down rather nervously, their faces broke into smiles, and in a body they came to greet me, calling out, "It is the English mademoiselle." They crowded round me, shaking hands and patting me on the back. Then they lined up and saluted, shouting: *"Vive Angleterre! Vive La France!"*

AFTERWORD

WHILE Beryl was translating the B.B.C. news to the assembled Frenchmen in the Siemreap Hotel, I had already been ordered back to India and was at that moment on my way to join a troopship, the *Duchess of Bedford*, about to sail from Greenock. I had sent a cable to Beryl at Loilem, the last post office in Burma on the road to Chieng Mai. Within 24 hours the reply had come back from the postmaster, "Regret lady left on foot for Siam." Thereafter the veil of security descended upon me and I could give her no information as to my movements, nor could I guess where she might be.

Beryl's story ends with the salute of the Frenchmen at the border post, and I am unsure how she got back to India but I remember that she told me that, having got back to India, she spoke to an old friend at Army Headquarters, the one that had climbed with us on our honeymoon, and asked him where and when I would arrive. He did not know but reminded her austerely that, in wartime, details as to the movement of ships were secret and that careless talk costs lives.

Leaving her address with my regiment, she went up to Gulmarg in Kashmir, where she had not been before, to await news of my arrival. She did not have to wait long. She had only been there a day when she passed two English "nannies", pushing their prams, and heard one say to the other, "They're expected back any day. They say that there are two big ships on their way, loaded with officers and civilians."

"So much for security," thought Beryl, and also that if there was any truth in this overheard rumour, I too must be on board. She left Gulmarg immediately and, on her way to Delhi, while stretching her legs on Lahore platform, she heard a dog barking excitedly in the guard's van. It was an Airedale; too hot, too closely confined and without water. She persuaded the guard to allow her to take it for a drink. A soldier stopped to talk to her and she explained the dog's predicament.

"But you must both come into my carriage," he said.

Beryl explained that she was travelling third class.

"How extraordinary," he said, "but never mind. I have a compartment to myself and I can fix it with the guard. Of course you must both come in."

Beryl found that he had something to do with Movement Control which explained his authority. When she and the dog were settled, she told him that she was hoping to meet me and that there were two ships said to be arriving. She asked if he knew at which port they would be docking.

"I haven't a clue," he said, "but as a long shot I'd try Bombay."

That was enough for Beryl. When she arrived in Bombay she went to Movement Control and asked when the ships would be arriving. She was told that they knew absolutely nothing about any ships. Nothing daunted, she went to a friend who was in business there and who had much to do with shipping.

"Of course," he said, "all the world knows about them. Every dhobi in Bombay has been alerted to be ready for the washing. They are doing the quickest turn-around in history and every contractor who ever supplied a ship knows the time and date of their arrival; the *Duchess of Bedford* and the *Britannic*." He told her that they would be docking on the following day and the quays at which they would be arriving.

As the *Duchess of Bedford* drew alongside the appointed quay, the ship was heeled with the weight of khaki-clad soldiers looking towards the shore. From boat deck to lower deck they thronged the rails, and a peculiar smell of sweat, overcrowding and badly washed clothes hung about us like a miasma. On the quay there were a few dock-hands, waiting to take our lines, a bevy of red-tabbed generals, and, standing apart from these, two girls: one of them — I could not at first believe my eyes — was Beryl. I shouted and waved as she scanned the rows of faces. Almost before she saw me and as the companionway was lowered, I fought my way to its head on a lower deck. As soon as it was made fast, I ran down it, brushing aside the General Officer Commanding Southern Command, the General Officer Commanding Bombay District and a brigadier or two as they made their way up the steps to greet the ship.

The whole ship's company cheered, and there were cries of, "Give her one for me!" and other ribald remarks, until a military policeman tapped me on the shoulder and said, "That's enough, Sir, back on board." Beryl followed me on board, wrinkling her nose and saying, "What an extraordinary smell." Shortly afterwards we were allowed ashore and next day started our journey to rejoin my regiment.

That was the end of her remarkable solo travels. We would be separated again by the war and come together again in many strange meetings and do many great voyages together, but never again would she be so completely alone, so carefree, so independent and so happily irresponsible as on the journeys that she has described in her previous book, *Winter Shoes in Springtime*, and in this one.

Miles Smeeton

Also by Beryl Smeeton

WINTER SHOES IN SPRINGTIME

Beryl Smeeton was that rare combination — an intrepid traveller, and a writer of entertaining prose — and she made astonishing journeys as a young woman in the 1930s. Going home alone, overland from India, mostly by bus and third-class train, she explored Persia (now Iran), where she was greeted with great kindness, and wangled an unusual trip through southern Russia. She then crossed Russia on the Trans-Siberian Railway with her brother (who, to her disgust, insisted on travelling first class) for a visit to Japan and Hong Kong. From there, on her most extraordinary trek, she roamed by riverboat, bus, train, truck and on foot through China and into Burma.

Later, Beryl married Miles Smeeton and brought to their adventures aboard *Tzu Hang* the same high energy, insatiable curiosity and sense of humour that shine through this, her delightful first book about her solo travels.